THE 50TH GATE

TRACKING OUR GROWTH THROUGH THE
COUNTING OF THE OMER

ALTERNADOX PRESS

Copyright © 2020 by Rabbi Gavriel Goldfeder

Original cover painting by Avraham Lowenthal
Book design by Karen Sperry Graphic Design

All rights reserved. Please do not reproduce all or part of this book without express consent of the author. If you have purchased an electronic copy, please print only for the personal use of the purchaser. For further information, please consult the 10 commandments, commandment number 8.

All inquiries about this and other Alternadox publications should be addressed to:

Rabbi Gavriel Goldfeder
heyrabbi@gmail.com
303 587 0701
www.alternadox.net
www.realrabbi.com

ACKNOWLEDGEMENTS

This book has grown through substantive learning and conversation with a wide array of interlocutors, including the Boulder Learning Group, the Omer Group at MIT, and the many wonderful people who have used the book and given feedback. In the end, though, this is the secret story of my own family. I am so grateful—really, I am—for how they push me to grow.

DEDICATION

In the merit of the Omer Work that we will do in and through this book, may we be purified and sanctified with top-level holiness. And through this may abundance flow into all worlds, to rectify our lives and spirits and souls from all dross and blemish.

INTRODUCTION

HUMAN INTERACTION is composite of seven elements called *sefirot* that serve as bridges or pipelines from ideation to expression. Each one of them must be in place and in good repair to ensure that our impulses to connect, to create, to help, and to support each other are implemented in the most positive and productive way.

These seven *sefirot* are brought into focus during the time of the Jewish year called the Counting of the Omer. In calendar time, the Counting of the Omer spans the seven weeks from the 16th of Nissan until the 5th of Sivan. In mythical time, these seven weeks connect leaving Egypt – the 16th of Nissan is the day after Passover – with the receiving of the Torah at Sinai (the 5th of Sivan is the day before Shavuot). Each of these seven weeks focuses on refining another *sefirah* so that, once we receive the Torah (which we do anew each year), we will be able to maximally manifest the Higher Will in the world.

In addition to the story of Passover-Shavuot and Exodus-Torah, Jewish tradition also tells of a tragedy that happened during these seven weeks:

> Rabbi Akiva had twelve thousand pairs of students… and they all died in one period of time, because they did not treat each other with respect… It is taught that all of them died in the period from Passover until Shavuot.[2]

With this narrative in mind, the Counting of the Omer has become a time of self-examination and personal growth, so that we might learn to "treat each other with respect." This respect is not simply offered or withheld; its content and expression are refined in several stages from ideation to expression in order to guarantee maximum positive impact. During the Omer, each stage along the way is given close attention for a week in order to ensure maximum positive impact.

But the Counting of the Omer does not only consist of seven weeks; it also consists of forty-nine days. The basic map of the seven *sefirot* is zoomed in on to reveal an even-more-detailed map of forty-nine sub-*sefirot*, whereby each *sefirah* is broken up into seven parts. Each of these seven parts is the focus of one day of the Omer.

[2] Talmud Bavli Yebamot 63b

The book you are holding describes the work for each week of the seven weeks of the Omer as well as each of the forty-nine days of the Omer, with a focus on relationships. All of our relationships – marriage, parenting, friendship, co-workers, rock bands, sports teams – call upon us to show up well, to give wisely and accurately, to be as aware as possible and as clear as possible, to take the right amount of responsibility, to push and pull, to speak and listen, to adjust and grow. These are the kinds of work that are outlined in this book.

* *

In doing the work of the Omer, a person might notice that they are really good at certain Omer-days, and have a harder time with others. Said another way, some of the skills outlined come more easily to some people, and other skills come more easily to others.

How would you know? Let's say you had a hard time on Day 21 of the Omer. Couldn't it be that you had a hard day on Day 21 of the Omer because that was when your car broke down, causing you to miss a crucial meeting? That may be. But how your day *went* – how you reacted, how you dealt with the situation, what happened next – is about you. And the "you" of that day can best be understood through the trait of that day (day 21 happens to be *malchut* of *tif'eret* – my wife's birthday). However it goes, this book allows you to jot down some notes on what came up, how you handled it, and what you learned along the way.

Fast forward to the next year. It would certainly be shocking if your car broke down on Day 21 of that year, too, and you once again missed a crucial meeting. But it is quite likely that something will happen that will call that day's trait back into focus, and you will be challenged by something that evokes an aspect of yourself that was evoked last year on that day. And, having counted the Omer and considered your notes from last year, you already had a lens and a vocabulary through which to observe yourself in context of that situation.

This version of *The 50th Gate* provides you with space to jot down some notes about each day of the Omer **over a five-year period**. As you count Day 21 of Year Two and Three and Four, you can look at what you figured out on that day in all previous years, and you can prepare yourself for how things might go this year. Forewarned is forearmed! Take your car in for a tune-up!

**

To use this book most effectively, begin counting the Omer on the second night of Passover, about half an hour after sundown. Start with the blessing:

Baruch Atah Ado-nai Elo-heinu Melech Ha'olam Asher Ki'de'shanu Be'mitz'vo'tav Ve'tzi'va'nu Al Sefirat Ha'Omer

Blessed are you, Ado-nai our God, Ruler of the World, Who sanctified us with commandments and commanded us concerning the counting of the Omer

Then you read the counting, at the top of each page. For example:

Hayom Asarah Yamim She'hem Shavua Echad V'shlosha Yamim La'omer

Then read the description of that day's trait. At the end of the day, jot down anything remarkable about your day – an insight you had, a challenge you faced, a victory you are celebrating, or a strength you didn't know you had, with whatever details you'd want want next-year-you to know. Next year, when you count, read last year's notes alongside the description of that day's trait.

You might add this prayer, which is found in many traditional prayerbooks:

Master of the universe, You have commanded us through Moses Your servant to count Sefirat Ha-Omer, in order to purify us from distracting elements and impurities. As You have written in Your Torah, "You shall count for yourselves from the day following the day of rest, from the day on which you bring the Omer as a wave-offering; [the counting] shall be for seven full weeks. Until the day following the seventh week shall you count fifty days," so that the souls of Your people Israel may be cleansed from their contamination. Therefore, may it be Your will, Ado-nai our God and God of our ancestors, that in the merit of the Sefirat Ha-Omer which I counted today, any blemish that I have caused in the *sefirah* of (**fill in the name of that day's trait**) be rectified, and may I be purified and sanctified with supernal holiness. And through this, may abundant bounty be poured out onto all the worlds. May it rectify all of our levels of soul from all dross and defect, to purify and sanctify us with Your supernal holiness. Amen, *selah*.

WEEK ONE
—
CHESED

Chesed is the willingness and capacity to be present and make contact despite unknowns, anxieties and uncertainties. It moves us closer to someone or something that needs love or attention. It has less to do with what we might give than it does with showing up and making contact. It may manifest as welcoming guests, as Avraham was known to do, but it requires more than just a meal.

Chesed is often mistranslated as 'kindness' or 'loving-kindness.' The association extends to the paragon of *chesed*, Avraham, who is usually thought of as a 'nice guy.' But this description does not sum up Avraham's contribution to the world. In Avraham's story, we certainly see evidence of his enthusiastic hospitality, but also so much more – and even some things that don't seem nice at all.

To understand *chesed*, we must look beyond generosity to what lies at the core of a gesture of welcoming. The essential ingredient in hospitality, and in Avraham's life of *chesed*, is taking the initiative to enter into unknown, uncomfortable, or difficult situations. For Avraham, this includes his courageous entrance into the land of Israel, his ability to initiate hard conversations, and even his commitment to the horrific Divine command to make his son into an offering.

The week of *chesed*, then, is about stepping into moments and situations and making meaningful contact, despite the temptation to stay in the safe confines of our own lives and spaces. *What* we give is secondary to the fact that we put ourselves in the vulnerable position of presence and caring.

WEEK ONE DAY ONE

Hayom yom echad la'omer

CHESED OF CHESED

Chesed of *chesed* is pure, unadulterated presence and love. It is the pure excitement of seeing someone you love whom you haven't seen in forever. There will be plenty of time later to catch up, to reminisce, and even to work out some issues that came up since you last saw each other. But for now, it's pure presence, contact, joy, and enthusiasm.

Chesed of *chesed* is not easy. It is something that children have. It is something a dog has when its owner comes home. We can lose touch with *chesed* of *chesed* as we take on more burdens of responsibility. And as relationships are complicated, we sense that it might be inappropriate to always show up in that way.

And yet *chesed* of *chesed* is the essential trait of the Omer. It is how I would *like* to show up if I didn't have to think about the mess the new puppy will make, or play it cool at the business meeting, or save money or think long-term: pure, unadulterated presence and love.

Consider Avraham. He has just been circumcised. He is sitting in his tent, recovering. Three strangers walk by. He knows (since he is the only monotheist around) that they are idolators. And yet, he *runs* to greet them and welcome them into his home. No concerns about their religious orientation. No thought to his recent surgical procedure. He runs.

Today we are asked: do we still have it in us? Or have we become so fixated on all those considerations – is there enough food? Am I busy? How much will it cost? What will the neighbors think? – that we can't let go and simply connect.

IN A SENTENCE
Connect. Pure and simple.

PRACTICE
Reach out to someone and allow yourself to feel and convey full openness (within the bounds of what is appropriate, of course). Don't worry about whether they are as open or excited as you are. Open your heart, your home, your wallet, your schedule – whatever you can do to make that person feel welcome and cared-for.

WEEK ONE DAY ONE

Reflections

YEAR ONE

YEAR TWO

YEAR THREE

YEAR FOUR

YEAR FIVE

WEEK ONE DAY TWO

Hayom shnei yamim la'omer

GEVURAH OF CHESED

Chesed of *chesed* implies willingness and capacity to be fully present, fully open, fully giving. It does not wait for cues as to what to give, or when. It gives everything, all the time, on all levels. *Gevurah* of *chesed* features the same willingness to make contact, but without filling the space. It moves into someone else's space or time, and waits.

Gevurah of *chesed* allows you to pick up the phone and call a friend you haven't seen for some time and say "Hey! I've missed you!" and then wait for a response. It lets a person know we are genuinely available but does not force a particular conversation. It simultaneously communicates caring along with respect for space, presence mixed with openness, contact without agenda, the loud and clear expression of proximity with the empowerment of silence. Active listening is a perfect example of *gevurah* of *chesed*.

IN A SENTENCE
Make contact, and then wait and listen.

PRACTICE
Reach out to someone, but focus on listening during that encounter. Figure out a way to let them indicate what they might need. When you find yourself filling in the silence, step back again.

WEEK ONE DAY TWO

Reflections

YEAR ONE

YEAR TWO

YEAR THREE

YEAR FOUR

YEAR FIVE

WEEK ONE DAY THREE

Hayom shelosha yamim la'omer

TIF'ERET OF CHESED

There are so many ways to be present for someone, and different situations call on us to show up in different ways. When going to a *shiva* house, for example, the best way to make contact is usually to sit silently and listen. This is very much *gevurah* of *chesed*. On the other hand, grabbing the bride or groom for a dance at the wedding may be the best way to show up — and this is more *chesed* of *chesed*. Both constitute stepping into other people's lives, but in ways that are appropriate to each situation.

Tif'eret implies a combination of *chesed* and *gevurah* that offers more than both of them put together. *Tif'eret* of *chesed* involves presence combined with flexibility. It calls for enthusiastic willingness to be in contact with others, coupled with flexibility as to what will be offered during the encounter. It conveys that I'm showing up with multiple options in hand, and I'm ready to offer all of them. That, in itself, can be reassuring.

The person sitting *shiva* might want to talk it up; maybe the bride and groom need a moment of quiet. *Tif'eret* of *chesed* jumps into the moment and listens for the next command, prepared to provide whatever is needed.

IN A SENTENCE
Make contact, ready to go in a few different directions.

PRACTICE
Make contact with someone and be prepared to push the interaction in a certain direction if necessary — or to let it go its own way if needed. Try to be mindful of how you approach the decision of what to do in that situation. Notice whether you leave enough space for the conversation or relationship to develop, or whether you quickly fill it with your own agenda and assumptions.

WEEK ONE DAY THREE

Reflections

YEAR ONE

YEAR TWO

YEAR THREE

YEAR FOUR

YEAR FIVE

WEEK ONE DAY FOUR

Hayom arba'ah yamim la'omer

NETZACH OF CHESED

To skillfully move through internal and external barriers so that *chesed* can come to fruition is the work of *netzach* of *chesed*.

Netzach is associated with power and perseverance to overcome obstacles for the sake of a long-term goal or vision. When focused internally, this trait responds to inner voices telling us not to visit a sick friend, make a *shiva* call, or volunteer at the soup kitchen because of the difficulty or awkwardness of these situations. *Netzach* of *chesed* challenges this resistance – perhaps by reminding us not to let a moment of potential awkwardness over-shadow the long-term importance of these acts.

There could be a thousand reasons why I can't make it over to my friend's house for a chat. I'd have to switch trains twice? Sure, that's real. But *netzach* of *chesed* allows us to persist through those obstacles in order to make contact.

IN A SENTENCE
When contact is definitely needed, *netzach* of *chesed* will make sure we get there.

PRACTICE
Who in your sphere needs more attention? Can you figure out what the barriers are to giving it? If the barriers are internal, give them a nudge and try to move past them. If they are external, be more assertive or creative in order to be present with that person, and see what happens.

WEEK ONE DAY FOUR

Reflections

YEAR ONE

YEAR TWO

YEAR THREE

YEAR FOUR

YEAR FIVE

WEEK ONE DAY FIVE

Hayom chamisha yamim la'omer

HOD OF CHESED

Hod is about seeing and appreciating the majesty of what is already present and available. *Hod* of *chesed* is deeper presence and stronger contact through recognition, appreciation, and reflection. "Wow! You've really worked hard to get where you are today!" as opposed to "We're almost there! Let's push a bit further!" It celebrates the beauty of the encounter itself – "it's so good to be talking with you!" – rather than focusing on what is preventing the encounter from becoming something more.

Unlike its brother *netzach*, *hod* is not directed toward a particular goal or purpose. Rather, *hod*'s purpose is the moment itself. Too much *netzach* of *chesed* makes us see situations as incomplete, defined by the obstacles that must be overcome. *Hod* of *chesed*, characterized by our capacity to see beauty in what is already at hand, provides counterbalance to that tendency.

So while *netzach* of *chesed* is about overcoming obstacles to loving presence and meaningful contact, *hod* of *chesed* involves creating an encounter through appreciating the beauty or logic of what already is – even the beauty of the barriers themselves.

Hod also honors advice and wisdom we can get from others. Has someone I know been in a similar situation? Can they offer me some advice about how to forge deeper contact in my relationships?

IN A SENTENCE
Instead of making contact in order to make change, make contact in order to appreciate.

PRACTICE
Reach out and make contact for the purpose of experiencing the relationship itself rather than with some goal in mind. Engage in a positive conversation, ready to celebrate the relationship itself rather than what it could become. Leave criticism at home. Bring humility, gratitude, and appreciation. This could be a good day to write a thank-you note.

WEEK ONE DAY FIVE

Reflections

YEAR ONE

YEAR TWO

YEAR THREE

YEAR FOUR

YEAR FIVE

WEEK ONE DAY SIX

Hayom shisha yamim la'omer

YESOD OF CHESED

Yesod honors both partners in a relationship. It involves the clarification and refinement of the relationship itself so that true *chesed* can be transmitted. Balanced *yesod* ensures that both people are seen, heard, nourished and satisfied. The opposite of *yesod* is extortion or subservience – using a relationship for one's own purposes or allowing one's self to be used.

With *yesod* of *chesed*, we observe how and why we make contact, and what happens to the relationship when we do. Being involved in the lives of others with the sole purpose of satisfying my own desires is a flaw in *yesod* of *chesed*. So is being involved in the lives of others at the expense of my own well-being.

Yesod of *chesed* makes us ask: am I making a *shiva* call because I want to be available, or because I want to score points in my community? Do I teach so I can feel powerful? Do I feel drained or used when I give? Am I trying to gain favor through generosity? Do people take advantage of me? Who receives when I give?

IN A SENTENCE
What happens to the relationship, and the people in it, around an act of *chesed*?

PRACTICE
As you make contact today, notice your motivations – are they truly generous? If not, what are you trying to gain? And when you do give, are your own needs being met? Is your giving really giving? Does the receiver appreciate it? Find out whether the person with whom you are interacting feels taken care of as well. Bring up the topic if it feels appropriate.

WEEK ONE DAY SIX

Reflections

YEAR ONE

YEAR TWO

YEAR THREE

YEAR FOUR

YEAR FIVE

WEEK ONE DAY SEVEN

Hayom shiva yamim she'hem shavuah echad la'omer

MALCHUT OF CHESED

Malchut implies a system of relationships organized around a certain principle. The ideal of *malchut* is a sovereign whose will is manifest without interference in all corners of the realm. Channels are fully open between will and expression.

If I can bring healthy, generative *chesed* to all the relationships that constitute my world, I have established *malchut* of *chesed*. But I may notice that I am able to manifest it only with certain kinds of people and not with others – with co-workers but not with family, with students but not with teachers, with friends but not with strangers.

Pretty much every encounter that I have can contain some facet of *chesed*. This will certainly look differently in each one, but just the same, there is most certainly a way for me to initiate healthy, appropriate contact. Today is the day to notice where this is or isn't happening, and to find some way to move forward.

IN A SENTENCE
In some relationships its hard for me to do *chesed*.

PRACTICE
Try to be and do *chesed* all day today. Look for ways to be present and involved with the people in your life – not nosy, not interfering, certainly not making people feel uncomfortable, but involved – to whatever extent you can manage, while maintaining your integrity and respecting their boundaries. Though not everyone is an Avraham, we are all his children, and we have it in us to care about each other and to share each other's concerns and joys.

WEEK ONE DAY SEVEN

Reflections

YEAR ONE

YEAR TWO

YEAR THREE

YEAR FOUR

YEAR FIVE

WEEK TWO

GEVURAH

Gevurah is epitomized by Yitzhak. A close reading of his story shows that he is almost always holding himself back – whether by allowing himself to be tied to the altar by his father or by not interfering with the lives of his sons.

The week of *gevurah* is marked by self-control and restraint. We know this from a classic line in Pirkei Avot – 'who is *gibbur* (same root as *gevurah*)? The one who controls their *yetzer* – inclination/tendency.'

Rebbe Nachman connects the word for inclination/tendency – *yetzer* – with the word *yetzirah* – formation. *Yetzirah* connotes forming something specific out of a raw material. Controlling the *yetzer*, then, implies holding back from manipulating what is before us – maybe for our own purposes, maybe because we think we know best, maybe out of impatience. *Gevurah*, then, is the capacity to *not* create – to wait, to allow.

Gevurah is thus one of the two most essential elements in life and relationship. While *chesed* is about stepping in and acting, *gevurah* is about holding back and allowing. So why does *gevurah* come after *chesed*? Because *chesed* is the point and the goal – we want to be involved and forward-moving, present and engaged. "The world is built upon *chesed*." *Gevurah* comes to ensure the accuracy, effectiveness, and sustainability of *chesed*. It is the temper, not the goal in itself.

WEEK TWO DAY ONE

Hayom shmonah yamim, she'hem shavua echad v'yom echad la'omer

CHESED OF GEVURAH

Chesed of *gevurah* initiates the creation of a space in which something can grow on its own terms.

Sometimes an outside force would interfere with a process that would otherwise produce useful results. *Chesed* of *gevurah* anticipates this interfering element and holds that outside force at bay.

A simple example is removing weeds so that another plant can grow. This serves as a powerful metaphor for all sorts of action to remove interference – separating two people who are hindering each other, removing oneself from a decision-making process because of bias, or removing a distracting device in order to get some work done.

IN A SENTENCE
Make a move to remove interference.

PRACTICE
Consider someone or something important to you – like your marriage, your family, your garden or schedule. What are your goals for the near future in that area? What's getting in the way? Pull out the 'weeds' – literally or figuratively. Are there things in your routine, like checking e-mail too often, that prevent you from using your time effectively? Actively interfere to keep those interferences in check.

WEEK TWO DAY ONE

Reflections

YEAR ONE

YEAR TWO

YEAR THREE

YEAR FOUR

YEAR FIVE

WEEK TWO DAY TWO

Hayom tesha yamim, she'hem shavua echad u'shnei yamim la'omer

GEVURAH OF GEVURAH

Today, two negatives make a positive. Sometimes we need to restrain our restraint, lest withholding action be interpreted as lack of caring. But there is a fine line between letting a situation move at its own pace and allowing the situation to spin off into chaos or disrepair. Consider the child who asks her parents whether she should buy a certain item with her money. There is a world of difference between, "Get whatever you want, it's your money" and "I wouldn't buy it, but I trust you to make a good decision. Let me know if you need more help thinking it through."

And there are situations in which, by trying to be too careful, we come off as stilted and artificial. When a warm greeting is needed, a careful "it is nice to see you" just won't cut it. Here, we need to check some of our restraint in order to unlock the exchange.

And sometimes, the weeds we are working so hard to remove aren't weeds. The things that keep threatening to interfere with our schedule might need our attention more than we thought. We might do such a good job clearing out the space that there is nothing left in it, and we might even forget the very thing for which we were trying to make space.

IN A SENTENCE
Make sure your restraint is constructive.

PRACTICE
Zero in on a relationship in which you are trying to give someone space – to make a decision, to find their own voice, to take initiative. Spend a moment considering what you are trying to accomplish in making that space. Are your distance and restraint helping reach that goal? Are they the right kind, and right amount, of distance and restraint? Might you need to make sure the person knows you are still there, and are rooting for them to succeed?

WEEK TWO DAY TWO

Reflections

YEAR ONE

YEAR TWO

YEAR THREE

YEAR FOUR

YEAR FIVE

WEEK TWO DAY THREE

Hayom asarah yamim, she'hem shavua echad u'shelosha yamim la'omer

TIF'ERET OF GEVURAH

Chesed of *gevurah* and *gevurah* of *gevurah* both emerge from the same intention – providing positive space to allow a person or situation to develop. *Chesed* of *gevurah* is active interference to hold obstacles – including your own opinions and "helpfulness" – at bay. *Gevurah* of *gevurah* ensures that you're creating the right kind of space, not stepping too far back or sending the wrong message when you step away.

Tif'eret of *gevurah* guides us toward finding a carefully nuanced expression of restraint within the range of *gevurah*. It puts us in the mode of 'attentive restraint,' continuously observing the situation and adjusting our approach so that our restraint is both caring and effective.

When our children are fighting, we have an opportunity for *tif'eret* of *gevurah*. If we allow them to slug it out on their own, they may come to think that no one will ever protect them. But if we interfere immediately, we are implying that someone else will always solve their conflicts. If, however, we actively observe the situation, jumping in before harm is done but allowing them to attempt to resolve the situation, we have flexed *tif'eret* of *gevurah*.

IN A SENTENCE
Space and restraint require constant attention in order to be done right.

PRACTICE
Consider a relationship in which your interference or withholding will directly affect the outcome of the situation. Find ways to let the involved person or people know that you are caring for them, without interfering. This can be done by asking questions, clarifying points, and nodding enthusiastically so the person knows you are paying attention. Notice how they respond to your restraint, and adjust accordingly. Be ready to take a step away or a step toward.

WEEK TWO DAY THREE

Reflections

YEAR ONE

YEAR TWO

YEAR THREE

YEAR FOUR

YEAR FIVE

WEEK TWO DAY FOUR

Hayom echad asar yom, she'hem shavua echad v'arba'ah yamim la'omer

NETZACH OF GEVURAH

Perhaps you know quite well what is preventing you from succeeding, or what you are doing that is preventing someone else from thriving, but don't yet have the courage or power to address the obstacles. That courage or power lies in *netzach* of *gevurah*.

Netzach always involves action or exertion for the sake of a greater vision. *Netzach* of *gevurah* focuses us on overcoming elements, attitudes and characteristics that prevent situations from playing out and people from growing, so that a greater vision can be realized.

The desire to help or connect is strong—and one that makes us human. So, we may have to fight our natural desire to connect or to help, when that desire would interfere with the larger goal. Such desires—whether driven by good will, love, anxiety, lust, impatience, good judgment, or religious ideals—tend to persist, despite our efforts to the contrary. A strong *netzach* of *gevurah* allows us to overcome ill-advised or ill-timed urges to connect, to assert, to interfere, or to force the world to conform to our vision.

Externally, we may find ourselves in relationship with someone who persistently asks for interference—like a child who asks for too much help in doing her homework or cleaning her room. We may have to help her past her fears—or her laziness—in order to help her understand the value of doing the work herself. This, too, is a function of *netzach* of *gevurah*.

IN A SENTENCE
Sometimes we have to exert some force in order to maintain space and restraint.

PRACTICE
Consider a situation in your life in which space is needed, and it is clear you are interfering too much. Your kid's homework? A workplace argument? A spouse's choices? Identify the internal and external factors that are pushing you to step over that boundary, and set your mind toward counteracting that urge.

WEEK TWO DAY FOUR

Reflections

YEAR ONE

YEAR TWO

YEAR THREE

YEAR FOUR

YEAR FIVE

WEEK TWO DAY FIVE

*Hayom shneim asar yom, she'hem shavua echad
v'chamisha yamim la'omer*

HOD OF GEVURAH

Hod is the partner/opposite of *netzach*. While *netzach* pushes through what is in the way, *hod* honors what is already there. *Netzach* of *gevurah* pushes away the obstacles that threaten the space that is needed for a situation to develop. *Hod* of *gevurah* is curious about what the situation is telling us. What kind of space is actually needed? How much? What, actually, is a weed?

We might think that our inner desire to give must be overcome in order to make room for someone else's development. And we might be convinced that the child asking for help with homework must be taught to be independent. But we might be wrong.

Today, we are listening: what is the person or situation trying to tell us about the way we withhold ourselves? Are we too far away? Are we doing it wrong? With *gevurah* of *gevurah* we tried to figure that out ourselves. Today, we're asking our partners-in-creation: how can I give you the best possible space? What are you trying to tell me?

And does someone else hold wisdom that can help me do this effectively? *Hod* is always willing to bring in advisors and to access their wisdom.

IN A SENTENCE
Listen so you can do better *gevurah*.

PRACTICE
Choose a relationship in which your interference or restraint is an important factor. Pay close attention to what s/he is telling you, verbally or not, about how your actions on that spectrum are affecting the relationship. Ask, if appropriate. Let that person tell you what they need in order to feel loved and allowed to grow at the same time.

WEEK TWO DAY FIVE

Reflections

YEAR ONE

YEAR TWO

YEAR THREE

YEAR FOUR

YEAR FIVE

WEEK TWO DAY SIX

Hayom shelosha asar yom, she'hem shavua echad ve'shisha yamim la'omer

YESOD OF GEVURAH

Today we explore how restraint is playing out within the relationships that matter. Refined *yesod* of *gevurah* guarantees that we feel respected by each other *and* in integrity with ourselves as we give – or are given – space. It is important that neither of us feels abandoned or powerless, over-stretched or under-loved, holding too much or holding too little. And this may call for patient explanation, deep listening, and other expressions of caring.

Space-making is tricky and sometimes hard to navigate. You shouldn't have to turn off my phone so I'll get my work done, but you should be allowed to suggest it. Similarly, I should not be blamed for your disappointing interview, but I should care enough to empathize when you tell me how frustrated you are.

If *yesod* of *gevurah* is properly tuned, the one who is more restrained is able to feel that that restraint is purposeful, positive, and even appreciated, and the one who is given space feels supported, trusted, and empowered.

IN A SENTENCE
Make sure the relationship served by *gevurah* is actually served by it.

PRACTICE
Is your restraint working? Is it creating better relationships? Notice how it sits with you: Are you frustrated? Relieved? Do you feel your restraint is understood and appreciated? Is it even seen as restraint? What other elements of the relationship need to be taken into account for it to be effective?

WEEK TWO DAY SIX

Reflections

YEAR ONE

YEAR TWO

YEAR THREE

YEAR FOUR

YEAR FIVE

WEEK TWO DAY SEVEN

Hayom arba'ah asar yom, she'hem shnei shavuot la'omer

MALCHUT OF GEVURAH

The *malchut* of each week of the *omer* points toward how well we can manifest that week's trait systemically. Put another way, are you able to turn this particular trait into a lifestyle, and not just manifest it occasionally, only with select people?

Malchut of *gevurah* challenges us to show healthy, appropriate restraint and self-containment in all aspects of our lives. It asks if we are focused and in control according to each situation. It challenges us to restrain ourselves from imposing our will or asserting our presence when those are not called for.

In our quest to apply *gevurah* systemically, we might notice that certain people or situations particularly challenge us in this area. Some people, for example, have a soft spot around children in need, and might interfere with the natural learning process because of their sensitivity to that issue. Others might be particularly challenged when the needed space is adjacent to their area of expertise.

IN A SENTENCE
Apply *gevurah* in all aspects of life, not just the easy ones.

PRACTICE
Now that you have worked through expressing *gevurah* in a proper way in one or two areas of your life, expand it. Go from work to play, from spouse to children, from co-workers to family. Notice patterns—where is it harder for you to do this? Why?

WEEK TWO DAY SEVEN

Reflections

YEAR ONE

YEAR TWO

YEAR THREE

YEAR FOUR

YEAR FIVE

WEEK THREE

TIF'ERET

The word *tif'eret* implies beauty, splendor, and harmony. It is the specific kind of beauty that comes about when disparate elements are thoughtfully combined.

This week challenges us to notice our strengths and shortcomings in how nuanced, rich, thoughtful, elegant and intricate we can be in our approach to situations. *Tif'eret* implies the capacity to create, cultivate and appreciate subtle, multi-faceted offerings and responses in a complicated world. After all, most situations require some admixture of generosity and restraint, expression and withholding, initiative and space, attention to my needs and attention to yours, concerns of the moment and concerns for the future.

The paragon of *tif'eret* is Ya'akov, who is called *'ish tam yoshev ohalim'* – the person who has 'integrity while sitting in tents.' The tents in which he sits are said to be the tents of Avraham his grandfather and Yitzhak his father. He learns from both of them. He carries their traits and approaches with him. But he is not fully defined by either of them. Rather, he understands that most situations call for him to weave them together.

WEEK THREE DAY ONE

Hayom chamisha asar yom she'hem shnei shavuot v'yom echad la'omer

CHESED OF TIF'ERET

Chesed of *tif'eret* initiates a complexification of a situation that has been made too simple, and to which cookie-cutter solutions no longer apply. This is not to be used everywhere, all the time. Some situations really are simple, and call for simple approaches and simple solutions. But many situations are not simple, and call for an approach and solution that reflect that complexity.

We should weave in additional elements when we see that simple solutions are not working, when an important voice is not in the conversation, when an important need is not satisfied, or when a greater beauty could be achieved if more colors are woven in.

Tif'eret is sorely needed in situations where rigid structures and opinions have replaced the fluidity that life requires. Some parents, for example, completely adopt only one parenting approach, often denying their own ambivalence as well as the uniqueness of different children. Similarly, people may adopt one approach to food or money that works most of the time but leaves some concerns unaddressed.

Whereas tomorrow's trait of *gevurah* of *tif'eret* involves restraint and space-making in order to allow beauty to emerge, today's trait is about initiating the process of identifying which voices and colors need to be included, and working toward weaving them in. It is about stepping closer to places of rigidity in hopes of reaching a deeper understanding of how nuance is possible.

IN A SENTENCE
Add more voices and colors when a situation has been overly simplified.

PRACTICE
What are the areas in your life where you struggle with flexibility, subtlety, or nuance? Consider ways to mitigate your monochromatic approach to those situations. Is there any wiggle room? Could you express your frustration with your child's behavior without sounding unloving? Could you express appreciation for someone without fully approving of everything they do? Can you find a way to enjoy eating without getting carried away?

WEEK THREE DAY ONE

Reflections

YEAR ONE

YEAR TWO

YEAR THREE

YEAR FOUR

YEAR FIVE

WEEK THREE DAY TWO

Hayom shisha asar yom she'hem shnei shavuot u'shnei yamim la'omer

GEVURAH OF TIF'ERET

With *gevurah* of *tif'eret*, we attempt to recognize that our very presence or expression may be impeding the emergence of other voices and colors. If this is true, we can actually encourage *tif'eret* by withdrawing or withholding. We may be the polarizing element, causing or pressuring those around us into one camp or another, emptying out the nuanced and beautiful middle realm. We should ask: would balance and harmony occur naturally if we were quieter, or even absent?

Today we are challenged to notice that sometimes *tif'eret* is initiated, and other times it naturally emerges. So we should listen for the subtle character of the people we meet and the situations we are in. Who or what is trying to be seen or heard? Who or what is being left out or shut out by the current approach? And what is my role in that?

IN A SENTENCE
Sometimes you are in the way of *tif'eret*. Learn how to step back.

PRACTICE
Notice what happens when you show up to the committees, relationships, boards, rock bands, or teams you are involved with. Does the mood shift? If you find ourself in a leadership position, ask just how much the situation really needs you to lead. Or are you being overbearing? Do your team members fear you, or think of you as a pushover? What can you do to make your presence there a contribution to the overall balance?

WEEK THREE DAY TWO

Reflections

YEAR ONE

YEAR TWO

YEAR THREE

YEAR FOUR

YEAR FIVE

WEEK THREE DAY THREE

Hayom shiva asar yom she'hem shnei shavuot u'shelosha yamim la'omer

TIF'ERET OF TIF'ERET

Tif'eret seeks to include a wide array of people, opinions, and considerations in our decisions and actions. It calls on us to move beyond the rigidity of binary responses, to incorporate – 'yes/and' – rather than reject – 'either/or' – when it is appropriate and productive to do so.

And yet, life often requires that we choose one action or another. I can't have lunch with you and not have lunch with you today. I can't take both jobs, or spend the same dollar twice. As I lay my dollar down, though, or sign on with one organization and not the other, I remain aware of the option I turned down. What am I to do with that sentiment?

Tif'eret in general guides me toward hearing all of the voices and factors as I make my decision and set my course. *Tif'eret* of *tif'eret* challenges me to include all those voices and factors even after I have made a yes/no decision.

For example, when I am considering whether to reach out to someone with whom I have been arguing, I may choose to do so – *chesed* – or not do so – *gevurah*. But *tif'eret* of *tif'eret* adds an ingredient that is absent from yeses and nos: it ensures that my 'no' can have a 'yes' in it, and my 'yes' can have a 'no' in it. That is, my reaction should reflect the variety and complexity of the factors in my decision-making process.

IN A SENTENCE
Even binary decisions can still hold complexity.

PRACTICE
When you make decisions today, be sure that as many factors as possible are represented in the answer. If you decide not to meet up for lunch, be sure that your desire to go is still expressed by scheduling another time to get together. Or offer a genuine expression of regret. If you cannot go to that wedding, write a personal note telling them how much you would have loved to go. And if you do decide to go, honor your own struggle with the time you'll miss at home by leaving when you need to.

WEEK THREE DAY THREE

Reflections

YEAR ONE

YEAR TWO

YEAR THREE

YEAR FOUR

YEAR FIVE

WEEK THREE DAY FOUR

Hayom shmonah asar yom she'hem shnei shavuot v'arba'ah yamim la'omer

NETZACH OF TIF'ERET

If my family is getting together to make a decision about our next vacation, I'm going to want to hear everyone's perspective. And I'm hoping to plan a vacation that will (by some miracle) satisfy as many needs and wants as possible. But if Child #2 never gets to talk because Child #1 has a loud tantrum and insists that it's her way or no way, then we have an obstacle to *tif'eret*. Some response is needed.

As we approach *netzach* of *tif'eret*, we enter the uncomfortable territory of having to push through obstacles in order to facilitate complexity, harmony, and balance. I will need to keep that obstacle in check without pushing it out of the picture. Meaning, the concerns that the obstacle raises are also real. They're just not the whole picture. Child #1 gets a voice, too, despite the tantrum.

With *tif'eret*, we are hoping for moments and situations in which a wide array of interests and elements can be woven together. Common internal obstacles to that goal include passivity, over-aggression, stubbornness, and other expressions of binary thinking. External obstacles could include everything from the noise in the room, time constraints, or lack of clearly articulated expectations for the range of the conversation.

With *netzach* of *tif'eret*, we notice the obstacles and consider what it would take to overcome them. And we also may notice whether we tend to overshoot our mark, with the *netzach* overcoming the *tif'eret* and becoming aggression.

IN A SENTENCE
Clear the obstacles to *tif'eret* out of the way. Push only as hard as necessary.

PRACTICE
Is there someone or something that is preventing the team or committee from operating in a balanced way? Can you address it directly without toppling the entire situation and negating the value of the obstacle? Is more structure needed? Perhaps someone is lacking important information? Whose voice is missing, and what needs to happen in order to bring it to the conversation?

WEEK THREE DAY FOUR

Reflections

YEAR ONE

YEAR TWO

YEAR THREE

YEAR FOUR

YEAR FIVE

WEEK THREE DAY FIVE

Hayom tisha asar yom she'hem shnei shavuot v'chamisha yamim la'omer

HOD OF TIF'ERET

So often, the balance we seek wants to emerge, or is already present, and only requires that we tune in to it. Whereas *netzach* of *tif'eret* is concerned with overcoming the barriers to beauty, complexity, and harmony, *hod* of *tif'eret* calls on us to recognize and be nourished by the *tif'eret* that is already there. In certain situations, rather than focusing on where *tif'eret* is absent, we should focus on how it is present, and then allow ourselves to be touched by it. And perhaps it is more present and pervasive than we thought.

Upon further investigation, we may find that the people and situations around us are far less rigid than we thought. Perhaps there are enough voices in the room and enough colors in the tapestry, and pushing to add more would result in chaos rather than complexity.

It may be that we need to challenge our own assumptions about how much nuance is needed here. Perhaps we are more rigid than we thought. Perhaps we are more interested in power than in beauty, and pushing to introduce more factors and voices is actually a way of asserting or retaining power. Or maybe we believe that we must always push to reach a higher plane. *Hod* of *tif'eret* calls upon us to relax, to be touched and nourished by the already-present richness of the situation.

And, *hod* always reminds us that we can tap teachers and mentors for wisdom and guidance. Maybe we are too "in it" and we can ask a trusted advisor for some perspective?

IN A SENTENCE
Tune into the rich beauty that is already happening.

PRACTICE
A walk through a forest may be the perfect opportunity to experience *hod* of *tif'eret*. In nature we find balance—life and death, growth and decay, patience and perseverance. And for this reason people often go into natural settings when we need to let go, relax, and gain perspective. Fully experience a situation where there is *tif'eret* so you can recalibrate. And then use that perspective to appreciate other areas in your life in which *tif'eret* might be there, but hidden.

WEEK THREE DAY FIVE

Reflections

YEAR ONE

YEAR TWO

YEAR THREE

YEAR FOUR

YEAR FIVE

WEEK THREE DAY SIX

Hayom esrim yom she'hem shnei shavuot v'shisha yamim la'omer

YESOD OF TIF'ERET

Not all *tif'erets* are *tif'erets*. Sometimes it looks like *tif'eret* is there – after all, multiple voices are represented, many colors are in the tapestry – but it is actually an uneasy peace, a balance that walks on eggshells. It could be that one or both of us is holding back for the sake of some fictional harmony of elements. Maybe we don't want to rock the boat, be a burden, or cause an inconvenience. Maybe we are scared.

When we have that big family meeting to plan our vacation, maybe kid #3 doesn't want to say anything, because everyone was excited about kid #2's idea, and kid #3 doesn't want to ruin the party. If that happens, we shouldn't be surprised if kid #3 doesn't have a great time.

So, what is the story of the relationships that produce our *tif'eret*? Is everyone able to contribute fully? Are people able to bring all of themselves to the mix? What if someone is too scared to speak? Or is forced to speak? These questions are addressed on the level of *yesod* of *tif'eret*. *Yesod* guarantees that we are all maximally aligned with the resultant *tif'eret* **and** with how we got there.

IN A SENTENCE
Be sure the foundations of harmony rest on mutual respect, freedom, joy and integrity.

PRACTICE
Consider a situation in your life in which there seems to be peace and balance. Find out if the balance is true, or if someone is withholding something they'd want to express. If you were more honest, would it shake the balance? Is someone being held hostage with this balance? Is someone worried about disappointing you?

WEEK THREE DAY SIX

Reflections

YEAR ONE

YEAR TWO

YEAR THREE

YEAR FOUR

YEAR FIVE

WEEK THREE DAY SEVEN

Hayom echad v'esrim yom she'hem shlosha shavuot la'omer

MALCHUT OF TIF'ERET

The goal is that *tif'eret* becomes a lifestyle. I want all of my relationships to hold as much *tif'eret* as is possible and appropriate. I want everyone in my life to bring as much of themselves to the mix as they feel comfortable doing. Likewise, I want to be able to bring as much of myself to the mix as I can.

Are there relationships in which that is clearly not happening? Is there a pattern that explains where *tif'eret* is happening more, and where it is happening less?

Maybe I have a hard time bringing *tif'eret* into self-care – food, sleep, downtime – while it's easier for me to bring it for others. Maybe my work relationships are too work-y and need to be balanced with a human touch. Maybe I'll discover that I don't know enough about what my kids are up to, and I need to make sure they feel comfortable talking about what's on their minds. What challenges tend to throw me off balance? When am I unable to offer a nuanced and thoughtful response?

IN A SENTENCE
Tif'eret everywhere.

PRACTICE
Choose an element in your life that seems rigid, binary, or out of balance. Get curious: Why is *tif'eret* not happening there? If you can consistently offer a balanced response in the context of your marriage, or around issues of work or play, work toward expanding that ability into another realm, like diet, your physical space, or your relationship with old friends.

WEEK THREE DAY SEVEN

Reflections

YEAR ONE

YEAR TWO

YEAR THREE

YEAR FOUR

YEAR FIVE

WEEK FOUR

NETZACH

Netzach means both victory and eternity. It represents the ability to continually push toward the fulfillment of long-term goals. This is likely to require that we deal with many obstacles along the way – internal and external. Moshe, the paragon of *netzach*, demonstrates a constant ability to deal with such obstacles persistently and creatively.

Moshe was charged with the task of liberating the Jewish people from under the hand of Pharaoh and Egypt, bringing them to Har Sinai to receive the Torah, and then leading them into the land of Israel. The challenges he met along the way were formidable. From the very beginning his mission met with resistance, from petulant demands for water and food to ideological challenges to his leadership. And yet Moshe continually marched forward on his mission to get the Jews to Israel. No stumble or misfortune ultimately set him off course, with the exception of hitting the rock. His loss of patience at that time was a failure on the level of *netzach*.

Moshe was not alone through this process. He was perpetually aided by Aharon the Priest, his brother. As we will see throughout the weeks of *netzach* and *hod* – of which Aharon is the paragon – these two work together constantly. Being all *netzach*, with a mentality that perfection is beyond the horizon, may cause everyone who falls short of the goal to feel like a failure. Being all *hod* – with the mentality that perfection is contained within that is happening now – leads to a lack of vision, mission or purpose.

Note that Moshe did not ultimately fulfill every element of the task with which he was charged: he did not succeed in bringing the Israelites into the land of Israel. This might teach us something important about *netzach*: namely, the ultimate vision I express in *netzach* may be unreachable. I might not get there. But constant movement toward that goal will define my life.

For this week, as grist for the mill, consider an element of your life that is like Moshe's: a multi-step process that involves other people who may not be completely on board with the mission, its pace, or how you are running it. How do people get on board? How do you keep moving? How do you not be demoralized? How do you not let setbacks set you back too far? How do you stay confident that your mission is worth pursuing? And, how do you make sure you're going at a pace that is likely to work for your people?

WEEK FOUR DAY ONE

Hayom shnayim v'esrim yom she'hem shlosha shavuot v'yom echad la'omer

CHESED OF NETZACH

Netzach kicks in as we begin to move forward with the plans we have. Of course it would be incredibly convenient to plan for everything that will happen along the way. But there are just so many kinds of obstacles, interruptions, challenges, and detours, and no one approach applies to all of them.

The only formula that covers all types of obstacles is that it is essential to know what is happening. And to know what is happening, one would have to get as close as possible to where the action is. That calls for *chesed* of *netzach*, which directs us to make contact with what is in front of us on the path, with questions like "what is this?" and "what might this have to do with the mission?" and "what does this tell me about how things are going, and what I might have to do?"

This contact needs to be made in a maximally unbiased way. We need to be as open as possible, genuinely able to hear all the feedback. We must be willing to admit it if it turns out that we are getting in the way of the fulfillment of our mission.

We should do *chesed* of *netzach* long enough to get clear on what's going on. If we have to ask more questions, we should ask more questions. If there is any way to get more data, we should collect as much as we can. We should use all of our senses, and mind and heart, in order to get the fullest sense of what is before us.

IN A SENTENCE

Check out what's in front of you as you move toward fulfilling your mission. Gather information. No ego.

PRACTICE

Pick a project or mission for which you are the convener or leader – one you could use for the entire week. It should be something more than 'my marriage' because marriages don't usually have leaders. But you could be the convener of the weekly money meeting, or in charge of getting the kids to clean up after dinner. Maybe you're the Minister of Fun. Whatever area it is, do some surveillance today. Scope out the situation – with maximum openness and empty ego. What's going on? Are you clear on the mission? Do you believe in it? Do you have a sense of what it will take to get there? Do you know how other people feel about it? Do people trust you? Do they care?

WEEK FOUR DAY ONE

Reflections

YEAR ONE

YEAR TWO

YEAR THREE

YEAR FOUR

YEAR FIVE

WEEK FOUR DAY TWO

Hayom shlosha v'esrim yom, she'hem shlosha shavuot u'shnei yamim la'omer

GEVURAH OF NETZACH

In *chesed* of *netzach*, you made contact with someone or something that will be a factor as you work toward fulfilling a mission that is under your auspices. You used that contact to gather info in as many ways as you could.

But it is not yet time to act. Rather, it is a time to *figure out* how to act. Flush with information, you can figure out the best way to take it apart, dissect it, graph it, draw it, plan it, format it, articulate it, or divvy it up. It is a time to go to the drawing board in order to make a plan based upon all that information. This plan or approach should include clear thinking on how we will deal with the "obstructions" on the path.

There are so many different levels—including timing and pace, mood and vibe, cost (social, time and money), and methods of communication. One must consider what they will need in order to make the plan work. Materials? Appreciation? More time alone? Feedback and input? Whose help could make this work? What are the different phases? How do they relate to each other? Maybe each of them will require a different vibe or approach.

IN A SENTENCE
With all the info you have, make a plan.

PRACTICE
That project that you chose to focus on this week: what do you now know? In whatever way works for you to chart it, chart it. If there's more info that you need, think about how you'll get it. Think about what your next couple of steps are and literally plan them. Notice the process of planning, as you go. Are you into it? Is it hard for you? And make sure you remember *why* you are doing all this. Sometimes *gevurah* forgets what it's about and gets lost in details.

WEEK FOUR DAY TWO

Reflections

YEAR ONE

YEAR TWO

YEAR THREE

YEAR FOUR

YEAR FIVE

WEEK FOUR DAY THREE

Hayom arba'ah v'esrim yom, she'hem shlosha shavuot ushelosha yamim la'omer

TIF'ERET OF NETZACH

With *tif'eret* of *netzach*, a person is in two worlds at once – connected to the people and elements that are part of the mission, and also well-situated in the command center. In *tif'eret* of *netzach*, a person will weave the path and the plan into a journey. They will move seamlessly between planning, calculating, communicating, thinking and shifting. Fully engaged and fully aware.

Remember that Moshe didn't spend all his time leading the people. He spent a lot of time communing with God or speaking with Aharon and his other students. Even at certain key moments when he was severely challenged, he stepped away from the people toward the Tent of Meeting in order to collect himself, after which he responded.

It is important to find the right flow between the command center – the Tent of Meeting, where all the charts and graphs and documents are – and the field where the people and the road reside.

IN A SENTENCE
Stay connected to the map and the terrain at the same time.

PRACTICE
That project or mission that you are working on this work this week: make sure you are not acting impetuously or angrily when there is a hitch. When you have to, go back and check in with your plans or advisors, and then make a good choice. Make sure you have the bigger picture – "the why" – in mind as you implement stages of your plan. Work on being fully present in each "location" – when you're with your people, be with them. When you're planning, be in planning.

WEEK FOUR DAY THREE

Reflections

YEAR ONE

YEAR TWO

YEAR THREE

YEAR FOUR

YEAR FIVE

WEEK FOUR DAY FOUR

Hayom chamisha v'esrim yom, she'hem shlosha shavuot v'arba'ah yamim la'omer

NETZACH OF NETZACH

Netzach of *netzach* is the exact middle of the Omer. It represents the transition between the inner world of thinking and planning and the outer world of action, relationship, and responsibility. A push is needed in order to make that move. *Netzach* of *netzach* is that push.

A contractor has checked out the terrain of the house she will be building. She knows about the terrain, the budget, the weather, and the team. She knows about her own costs, the dynamics within that team, issues around timing, client expectations, and everything else she can know. And now it is time to begin. At some point, the hammer will have to hit the first nail.

Netzach of *netzach* pushes against the sense that I have to plan more, gather more intel, talk more, or even pray more. In one key moment in Moshe's leadership, as the Israelites stood before the Red Sea, God says, "Why are you crying out to me? Tell the Jewish people to move forward!"

It is important to know that "forward" does not have a particular size-of-task associated with it. It may well be that the big first step in *netzach* of *netzach* doesn't actually look like a great, glorious step forward. It could require getting this nail pounded into exactly the right place, or writing the perfect piece of code, or giving any one detail all of one's attention. This is in fact moving forward, and one would have to be patient enough to know that this is what needs to happen, and therefore IS moving forward. Remember that Moshe didn't think talking to the rock was an important-enough detail. Don't hit the rock.

On the other hand, it may be that this thing shouldn't get to slow you down or deter you. It may be that you're fixated on something that doesn't matter nearly as much as it seems. *Netzach* of *netzach* could give you the clarity to side-step, blast through, or ignore.

IN A SENTENCE
Time to take a real step forward, no matter how small it seems.

PRACTICE
Make sure that project isn't stagnating. You stand on the border between planning and action, between inner and outer. Time to make a move, even if the move seems small or insignificant. And when you do, commit to it, deeply and thoroughly, until it is done.

WEEK FOUR DAY FOUR

Reflections

YEAR ONE

YEAR TWO

YEAR THREE

YEAR FOUR

YEAR FIVE

WEEK FOUR DAY FIVE

Hayom shisha v'esrim yom she'hem shlosha shavuot v'chamisha yamim la'omer

HOD OF NETZACH

Hod of *netzach* (today) and *netzach* of *hod* (day 32) represent the interactions between the elements embodied by Moshe and Aharon. Moshe and Aharon held quite different – and equally essential – leadership roles for the Jewish people. While Moshe was primarily responsible for receiving the vision from God, communicating it to the people, and keeping everyone moving toward the fulfillment of that vision, Aharon was tasked with picking the people up when they fell short of the vision. Moshe pushed people to perfection, while Aharon helped people stay connected amidst their imperfections. Moshe brought the perfect vision from heaven down to earth, while Aharon brought imperfect people back up to contact with God.

Today we are challenged to hold these two agendas at the same time. We continue to keep ourselves and our people on task. And, along the way, we should be celebrating victories, calling attention to beauty, and offering gratitude and recognition. We must resist the urge to look at what is happening only in terms of the plans we have made, the metrics we have laid out, the standards we hold by, and whether or not people can measure up to them.

Rather, along the way, *hod* of *netzach* calls on us to see and appreciate the beauty that shines out as we go. Those moments of glory and transcendence have value in themselves, independent of whether and how they fit into the fulfillment of the larger plan.

IN A SENTENCE
Stay committed to your mission, and enjoy and appreciate what is happening along the way.

PRACTICE
Now that *netzach* of *netzach* has pushed you into motion, look around. Remember that your mission is important, but it is not everything. There are other missions happening, other centers of meaning, other processes in which you are following and not leading. So get context for what you are doing, and remind yourself of the bigger picture. Enjoy yourself!

WEEK FOUR DAY FIVE

Reflections

YEAR ONE

YEAR TWO

YEAR THREE

YEAR FOUR

YEAR FIVE

WEEK FOUR DAY SIX

Hayom shiva v'esrim yom, she'hem shlosha shavuot v'shisha yamim la'omer

YESOD OF NETZACH

As Moshe marched the Israelites to the land of Israel, one of his goals was the transformation of the people he was leading. Not only did he want them to walk, he wanted them to believe. He wanted them to grow, and to be transformed by the process.

I would assume that our missions are far more pedestrian, and far less evangelical. And yet, don't we hope that our relationships will be transformed by the process? That through this process, we will know each other better, trust each other more, be more capable of building healthy boundaries, and be more attentive to communication?

And, even further: Don't we hope that the process of working toward fulfillment of our missions will give us increased self-confidence, a more positive self-image, a better awareness of what we're good at and a sense of what kinds of help and support we need?

Yesod of *netzach* brings our relationships into focus as we move forward and manage obstacles. Some of those obstacles may occur between us and the people with whom we are working. *Yesod* of *netzach* asks us how we are handling the relationships. Are we able to get people on board with our mission? Is the mission getting in the way? Is it enhancing the relationship?

IN A SENTENCE
How are your relationships as you do your mission?

PRACTICE
Spend some time considering the mission on which you are focusing this week. Now consider the relationships that make it work, or hold it up, or give it purpose. How have those relationships changed? What happens when one of your important relationships includes an obstacle to your mission? Is it confusing to prioritize one or the other? How can you maintain your commitment to your mission and to your relationships at the same time?

WEEK FOUR DAY SIX

Reflections

YEAR ONE

YEAR TWO

YEAR THREE

YEAR FOUR

YEAR FIVE

WEEK FOUR DAY SEVEN

Hayom shmonah v'esrim yom she'hem

MALCHUT OF NETZACH

Malchut, as always, challenges us to make something local and specific into something ubiquitous and systemic. Until now in the week of *netzach*, we have chosen a project or a slice of life in which we can implement a mission. We have practiced the craft of gathering information, of creating a plan, of weaving together the plan and the world it addresses. We have observed what this does to our relationships, and how we can be present and alert along the way.

With *malchut* of *netzach*, we broaden our scope to questions like: where is *netzach* being demanded of us? Where else can—or must—we implement our *netzach* skills? This week we chose a *netzach*. Is there a *netzach* that is choosing us?

We might have chosen to work on getting the kids to do chores, planning a vacation, developing a budget, or facilitating an important conversation at work. But maybe those were relatively safe choices. Are we being called upon to engage with much larger missions—earn another $50,000 this year, or put this product into 100,000 households, or run for city council to address local homelessness?

Too big? Remember that Moshe did not succeed in bringing the Israelites into the land of Israel. He brought them *up to* the land of Israel.

A mission may well be something that we will not complete. And yet, in the words of Pirkei Avot, "It is not upon you to finish the work. And you are not free to desist from it."

IN A SENTENCE
Is there a bigger *netzach* for you?

PRACTICE
Open to the question of what is being demanded of you. What do other people think your mission should be? What is needed in your household, your community, your place of worship, or your place of work? This does not mean you must take everything—or anything—on. But allow yourself to be moved by the question. If another—or bigger—*netzach* draws you in, consider beginning again with *chesed* of *netzach* on that new project or mission.

WEEK FOUR DAY SEVEN

Reflections

YEAR ONE

YEAR TWO

YEAR THREE

YEAR FOUR

YEAR FIVE

WEEK FIVE

HOD

THE WORD *HOD* IMPLIES majesty and beauty and is epitomized by Aharon the Priest. Though he certainly looked resplendent in his priestly robes, this is not the reason for the association. Rather, Aharon's *hod* emerges from his ability to find majesty and beauty in others — even (and especially) in those who stumble and fall.

Aharon was the High Priest — advocate, therapist, cheerleader, healer, and so much more. While his brother Moshe brought the perfect Divine vision from heaven to earth, Aharon the Priest brought broken people up to heaven. He helped them love themselves even when they seemingly failed in pursuit of perfection. He appreciated their uniqueness and their struggle. He reflected the beauty of people who had lost their own sense of it. And none of this could be done without real and genuine humility. If he did not actually see their majesty, he could not convince them that it was there.

The week of *hod* calls upon us to recognize and make space for others even when it does not seem to fit with our vision; even when it challenges our assumptions as to what constitutes success.

This week is the converse and complement of last week's work in *netzach*, which described our ability to assert ourselves in the world. *Netzach* is about pushing toward the future; *hod* involves seeing majesty in the present, and being open to receiving and honoring it.

WEEK FIVE DAY ONE

Hayom tisha v'esrim yom she'hem arba'ah shavuot v'yom echad la'omer

CHESED OF HOD

Chesed of *hod* is the tool we use to actively put ourselves in a state of receiving, humility, openness and respect. With this 'active *hod*' we do not wait for someone else's light to burst into our line of vision. We do not wait for a reason to see and appreciate beauty and quality.

Hod is not something we reluctantly do because our mission has failed. We must develop *hod* independently of how things are going and what is happening around us. And in so doing, we make normal moments into moments of relationship and learning. As we do so, we might be giving someone the gift of being allowed to shine.

When the attitude of *chesed* of *hod* is well-developed, we have a natural capacity and tendency to be blessed by what is happening around us—even the smallest of things. We become proactive appreciators.

This trait may be useful when we can anticipate being in a learning situation, like attending a class, or when we are about to enter an important conversation with a business partner or loved one. At such times, we can enter into a *hod* mindset preemptively.

And *chesed* of *hod* helps us ask for advice when we need it. Maybe someone else has a better angle from which to see the beauty we're not seeing.

IN A SENTENCE
Before you do what you're about to do, open up.

PRACTICE
Spend some time preparing to appreciate, respect, and learn from people even before you are with them, so that when you are with them, you'll be ready to receive from them. When you find yourself judging other people for falling short in your eyes, work on switching to the role of fan, advocate, or cheerleader. Remember, even the smallest accomplishment is worth celebrating.

WEEK FIVE DAY ONE

Reflections

YEAR ONE

YEAR TWO

YEAR THREE

YEAR FOUR

YEAR FIVE

WEEK FIVE DAY TWO

Hayom sheloshim yom she'hem arba'ah shavuot ushnei yamim la'omer

GEVURAH OF HOD

Some people shouldn't be listened to or learned from. *Gevurah* of *hod* implies withholding *hod* where it might lead to disillusion and distortion.

Hod can be idolatrous when we humble ourselves before that which is not worthy of it. Yes, everything has good in it. But we might not be capable of receiving it, and the giver might not be capable of giving it without major strings attached.

Misplaced *hod* can taint the character of an interaction by inappropriately or prematurely turning someone into the teacher, provider or visionary. If I approach a scoundrel with *hod* I may regret it. So even if I see it, I may need to keep my appreciation to myself.

Where *hod* can become flattery, and where expressions of gratitude will give the recipient a false sense of accomplishment, *gevurah* of *hod* may be needed. We may need to withhold our feelings of appreciation, even if we feel it deeply, because it would be counterproductive to express them.

Though I do not want to approach every situation with caution or cynicism, I must have in my toolbox the capacity to withhold *hod* for the greater good.

IN A SENTENCE
Sometimes it is best to keep your appreciation or admiration to yourself.

PRACTICE
Am I giving attention, power, a platform, positive feedback or affirmation to someone who is not served by it right now, or doesn't deserve it, or might even use it against me? Am I flattering someone by expressing gratitude that I don't feel because I want something from them, or because I am afraid of them?

WEEK FIVE DAY TWO

Reflections

YEAR ONE

YEAR TWO

YEAR THREE

YEAR FOUR

YEAR FIVE

WEEK FIVE DAY THREE

Hayom echad u'sheloshim yom she'hem arba'ah shavuot ushelosha yamim la'omer

TIF'ERET OF HOD

When *hod* is offered too freely it can be unsafe. When it is withheld too strongly it can project disrespect, coldness, or defensiveness. We are often challenged to find the balance by showing that we are willing to give *hod* while maintaining our right and capacity to give it in a way that makes sense to us. We thus come across as neither arrogant or naive. Rather, we are thoughtful and alert.

Aharon the Priest must have been challenged in this realm. His job was to let people see how wonderful they are, and to provide empathy and support for people in their struggles, but he would have to do so without endorsing ill-advised decisions. And yet, if he withheld those nourishing expressions too strongly he would be perceived as judgmental, and this would have proven antithetical to his ultimate purpose.

To master this tool is to master the balance of how, and how much, to let go of goals and vision and embrace the reality before us. With this trait we hold *hod* in hand, willing and prepared to express it as soon as we are clear that it is appropriate and capable of withholding it when necessary.

The more fine-tuned our *tif'eret* of *hod* is, the more others will feel both appreciated and inspired to keep growing.

IN A SENTENCE
Express the right amount of appreciation and admiration. There is beauty here, and I've still got concerns.

PRACTICE
Look at some of your relationships more closely in terms of how you express humility, respect, and appreciation. Are you in control of your *hod* in that relationship, or does it have a mind of its own? Consider how and how much *hod* you give. Why is it so? Are you actively deciding how and how much to express it?

WEEK FIVE DAY THREE

Reflections

YEAR ONE

YEAR TWO

YEAR THREE

YEAR FOUR

YEAR FIVE

WEEK FIVE DAY FOUR

Hayom shnayim ushloshim yom she'hem arba'ah shavuot v'arba'ah yamim la'omer

NETZACH OF HOD

Not surprisingly, some people have a hard time seeing that they, too, have light inside. People and situations often resist revealing their power, soul, beauty, majesty or wisdom. This happens for many reasons, including fear, shyness, past rejections, shame, and anxiety about power. Sometimes, then, it is our job to facilitate others' capacity to shine, to express, to give and to teach. And we may need to push a bit.

Whereas *netzach* of *netzach* describes pushing through obstacles that stand in the way of our own vision and mission, *netzach* of *hod* implies pushing through obstacles to others' shining and expression. At the root of *netzach* of *hod* is belief that the people around us have wisdom or beauty or love to give, even if it is yet to be revealed. Today we take upon ourselves to identify and help remove obstacles to other people's realizations and revelations of wisdom, soul, power, beauty and goodness.

And one of the obstacles could be that we don't want to call in outside help in order to see it. We might feel our own shame at not seeing the good in someone we love. We'll need to push past that resistance.

IN A SENTENCE
Push barriers out of the way so that other people can shine.

PRACTICE
Consider a relationship in which you are not seeing beauty, not receiving wisdom, or not being nourished. What's in the way? Is your judgment a factor? What could you do to allow their *hod* to shine forth, to teach you and inspire you? Is there someone who can help you do it, but you don't want to ask for help? Work toward removing those obstacles.

WEEK FIVE DAY FOUR

Reflections

YEAR ONE

YEAR TWO

YEAR THREE

YEAR FOUR

YEAR FIVE

WEEK FIVE DAY FIVE

Hayom shelosha ushloshim yom she'hem arba'ah shavuot v'chamisha yamim la'omer

HOD OF HOD

Today is a day of faith, because it is one of the most passive days of the Omer. While *netzach* of *hod* implies the capacity to actively help others see and express their own beauty, *hod* of *hod* requires standing back to allow the beauty of a person or situation to emerge and express itself, in its own way and at its own pace. My only jobs: don't interfere and open up. This requires faith that the goodness and wisdom and soul of the situation are actually there and do not require my interference.

Today is Lag B'Omer, the commemoration of the death of Rabbi Shimon bar Yochai, to whom the Zohar is attributed. He was the ultimate mystic who made himself into a completely open vessel for the inner light of the Torah. He models how to stand in front of a person, a text, or a moment with full faith that it contains light that doesn't need our pushing in order to shine. And inasmuch as we can humbly assume the stance of being a vessel, the source will fill us with its light.

So when I am standing in a situation today that doesn't immediately inspire me – sitting in a waiting room, paying the bills, attending a not-quite-interesting class – my work is to open, believe, and wait. If I am truly humble, the light that is here will ultimately reveal itself. And if I already see the beauty, I can open further to behold even more beauty.

IN A SENTENCE
Open. And open again.

PRACTICE
Stop trying to fabricate someone's goodness or beauty or brilliance, and open yourself up to the true beauty that is already there. Don't make up stories about why a situation is good – open to it until its goodness becomes clear to you on its own terms.

WEEK FIVE DAY FIVE

Reflections

YEAR ONE

YEAR TWO

YEAR THREE

YEAR FOUR

YEAR FIVE

WEEK FIVE DAY SIX

Hayom arba'ah u'shloshim yom she'hem arba'ah shavuot v'shisha yamim la'omer

YESOD OF HOD

People are sensitive about seeing their own beauty and about feeling that they have something to give, and not every gesture toward helping unleash those gifts will be successful or well-received. There are many reasons why this is so, but one important factor is our own motive.

Why do I want you to shine? Why do I want you to bring your gifts forth into the world? Maybe I want it for me – I want you to shine because I want what you have to give. Or maybe I want you to shine for you, because I want you to know that you've got it in you.

Both of those are part of the picture.

Yesod of *hod* challenges us to find the balance between my needs and yours relative to the beauty, knowledge, and love that you have inside. If I base my actions entirely on my needs I may lose a sense of the boundary between gift-receiving and extortion. I might get impatient, and that won't help anyone. But if I ignore my own needs, I might be less motivated to engage, and you might not believe that you actually have something useful to offer.

Yesod of *hod* calls upon us to be sure we are not using people for their gifts and that, at the same time, we are genuinely interested in receiving them. We must be sure that the other person's shining and giving is as satisfying to them as our receiving is to us.

IN A SENTENCE
How's our relationship, as I try to support you to shine? Are we both happy?

PRACTICE
Think of a few people in your life. Take a good look at whether and why you want them to manifest their beauty, knowledge, or love. Do you want others to shine, or do you want to be the only one? When they do shine, are you willing to be affected by it? Are you able to express gratitude and appreciation at those moments?

WEEK FIVE DAY SIX

Reflections

YEAR ONE

YEAR TWO

YEAR THREE

YEAR FOUR

YEAR FIVE

WEEK FIVE DAY SEVEN

Hayom chamisha ushloshim yom she'hem chamisha shavuot la'omer

MALCHUT OF HOD

Malchut challenges us to make a particular skill or attitude systemic. Though we might use a particular kind of moment or relationship as a case study, we must ultimately learn to apply these important principles to the widest range of situations and relationships.

For *malchut* of *hod*, we are challenged to open to majesty, goodness, wisdom, and beauty from a wider array of sources. Some people, places, and situations are easy for us. It's not hard to have *hod* with our kids, or in a forest, or listening to Gould's Brandenburg Concertos. So what about our parents, or city streets, or whatever music our kids listen to?

Maybe heart-space is easy for us. What about mind? Maybe it's easy to learn from teachers. How about learning from fellow learners, or from students? Maybe it's easy for us to take advice from someone with a diploma on the wall or a best-selling self-help book. What about graduates from the school of hard knocks? And how good are we at appreciating our own wisdom?

Today is an opportunity to ask: Which are the relationships within which we tend to exercise healthy *hod*, and which are the ones that are more challenging for us? With that knowledge in hand, we can move forward in discovering the underlying causes and effects of how we do *hod*, and to make a move in a positive direction.

IN A SENTENCE
Find more beauty in more places and in more people.

PRACTICE
Look around. Who or what, by your current estimation, has no light to shine and nothing to share? What makes you so sure? Take a step toward evoking that person or situation's inherent beauty. Remind yourself that Aharon saw real majesty in everyone, even people who wanted to worship a gold cow, and Rabbi Shimon bar Yochai could find it everywhere, too.

WEEK FIVE DAY SEVEN

Reflections

YEAR ONE

YEAR TWO

YEAR THREE

YEAR FOUR

YEAR FIVE

WEEK SIX

—

YESOD

RABBI ARYEH KAPLAN DEFINES the refinement of *yesod* as a balanced experience of giving and receiving nourishment and pleasure. When *yesod* is aligned, both partners-in-relationship are satisfied, respected, seen and heard. Needs are acknowledged and honored. Any giving that happens is balanced and appropriate. Appreciation is expressed. This is called *tikkun habrit* – when the commitment between two people is clear, rectified and healthy.

When *yesod* is out of alignment, one or both partners may be using the other for selfish purposes, or overly sacrificing their own needs in order to please the other. In either case, one or both becomes less than a full individual. They are reduced to their role as pleasure-provider. This is called *pegam habrit* – a breakdown of the agreement, spoken or unspoken, that allows for selfish pleasure-seeking to replace the pursuit of mutual satisfaction.

These ideas of rectified or broken covenant manifest in any and every realm of communion and communication – including sexuality and speech. These are two of the most intimate ways in which people interact, and are therefore two realms in which our level of *tikkun habrit* will be most obvious. But what is revealed in sexuality and speech is often an expression of deeply-held assumptions about how the entirety of a relationship should go.

Refining *yesod* may be the most difficult work of the *omer*. It deals with core issues of self-centeredness, self-worth and self-respect, dependency and abandonment, generosity and seeing the other, the limits of awareness, and the challenges of engaging in full and honest relationship.

The week of Yesod is supported by Rabbi Avi Rosenfeld in honor of his wife Rachel and their son Michael Yehuda who was born on Malchut sh'b'Yesod in Yerushalayim.

WEEK SIX DAY ONE

Hayom shisha u'sheloshim yom, she'hem chamisha shavuot v'yom echad la'omer

CHESED OF YESOD

Chesed of *yesod* pushes us to bring relationship into the center of our awareness. It challenges us to bring the dynamics of our relationships into focus, so that we can bring them into balance. *Chesed* of *yesod* demands that we pay attention to the questions we may not want to ask ourselves – or each other.

In context of this trait, we pay attention to how we talk. We observe ourselves as we interact with others – are we both allowed to bring our concerns to the table? Does one of us get to talk more than the other, or have his or her needs met more often or more thoroughly?

At certain points, it becomes essential to address foundational questions of how we relate and communicate. But it is easier, and less scary, to talk about particular situations than to talk about the structures and assumptions underlying those situations. For example, arguing about whose dishes are littering the counter is far easier than talking about how we decided who should be doing the dishes in the first place. But today we bring those underlying dynamics into focus so we can get closer to balance.

IN A SENTENCE
Why are your relationships the way they are?

PRACTICE
Choose one of the important relationships in your life and begin the process of observing how that relationship goes. Be open to hearing that there is work to be done, and that you might not be showing up (or allowing him or her to show up) as fully as possible. Consider bringing up your observations or concerns about that relationship, with an openness toward understanding your role in how things are going, what got you to that place, and what some other options might be.

WEEK SIX DAY ONE

Reflections

YEAR ONE

YEAR TWO

YEAR THREE

YEAR FOUR

YEAR FIVE

WEEK SIX DAY TWO

Hayom shiva u'sheloshim yom, she'hem chamisha shavuot ushnei yamim la'omer

GEVURAH OF YESOD

Sometimes people are out of sorts, tired, frustrated, or lacking emotional and energetic resources, and it is not useful to use that moment as an indication of the state of that relationship. Resisting the urge to render judgment on or process about relationship at the wrong time is an essential skill to develop, and today it comes in to focus.

Judaism is no stranger to limiting certain expressions of relationship to very specific times and places. There are certain times when we are encouraged to engage in reflection relationship on, and hopefully improvement of, relationship. And much of the time we need to simply *be* in relationship. If we analyze too much, imagine other possibilities too much, and talk about it too much, all this processing will one day replace the relationship itself and leave us alienated from ourselves, each other, and the bond that connects us. It is quite possible to become too self-conscious.

Thus, restraint is absolutely necessary in this realm. When we see that there is too much stress or things are too out-of-sorts we should focus on loving and giving, not analysis. And when we see that talk won't help, we need to refrain from talking about it. It is a violation of *tikkun habrit* to make someone talk just because we want to have that conversation.

IN A SENTENCE
There will be a time to talk. Patience.

PRACTICE
Notice relationships or situations in which you over-assess, over-process or over-talk. What makes you do it? Is there an alternative approach? How you can put a stop to it? What can you replace over-processing with? Could this be a time to just be present? Maybe prayer?

WEEK SIX DAY TWO

Reflections

YEAR ONE

YEAR TWO

YEAR THREE

YEAR FOUR

YEAR FIVE

WEEK SIX DAY THREE

Hayom shmona u'sheloshim yom, she'hem chamisha shavuot u'shelosha yamim la'omer

TIF'ERET OF YESOD

Tif'eret and *yesod*, which both occupy the 'middle column' of traits, are about balance and nuance. While *tif'eret* addresses balance in terms of what I bring to the table, *yesod* balances what happens at the table. Today we are trying to find balance between our need to focus on or work on relationship with our awareness that it may not be the right time, or that we might not yet have the skills to do so.

I am therefore challenged to hold both considerations: how can I notice the dynamics of our relationship with an eye toward improvement – without stepping out of relationship in order to do so? How can I make sure my willingness to overlook – or not mention – certain elements is a willful expression of love and maturity, and not an expression of the problem itself?

The people associated with *tif'eret* and *yesod* are Ya'akov and Yosef, respectively – father and son. Yosef embarked on a journey of relationship, in search of the proper balance between expressing power and withholding it. Ya'akov gave Yosef the good judgment that would allow him to do so. He taught him about the inner balance that would ultimately ensure outer balance.

IN A SENTENCE
Even when there's work to be done, use your best judgment to figure out if it's a good time.

PRACTICE
Which relationship is most live for you today? Consider whether today is a good day to note the dynamics of the relationship, whether a conversation about those dynamics is possible, and what would make it go well. But before you engage so directly, consider whether you are clear on what you want to accomplish by engaging. Take a good look at your own sense of balance going into any conversations that ensue. Are you clear and relaxed enough to have that talk?

WEEK SIX DAY THREE

Reflections

YEAR ONE

YEAR TWO

YEAR THREE

YEAR FOUR

YEAR FIVE

WEEK SIX DAY FOUR

Hayom tisha u'sheloshim yom, she'hem chamisha shavuot v'arba'ah yamim la'omer

NETZACH OF YESOD

Sometimes it feels a lot easier and safer to avoid noticing or working on the dynamics of a relationship. But an incapacity or unwillingness to do so can leave us swimming in cycles of dysfunction, delusion, or boredom. It is therefore important, at certain moments, to break through the barriers that prevent us from looking, discussing, or adjusting.

But, like every expression of *netzach*, this "breaking through" needs to be done with utmost care. After all, out-of-control *netzach* is the very antithesis of *yesod* because it favors one person's perceived needs at the expense of another's. *Netzach* of *yesod* thus challenges us to, when appropriate, push past the barriers that prevent us from recognizing, discussing, and adjusting elements of relationship for our mutual benefit. To do this right, the very act of overcoming obstacles must actually serve the relationship and not threaten it. The means and the ends must be aligned. And a key part of that is not pushing *myself* to have conversations I'm not ready for.

We are in very sensitive territory here. It is hard to look at relationship, and harder to change it. We may notice things we didn't think we wanted to see. Having effective and generative conversations in this realm seems to require the skill of a surgeon. Perhaps this is why so many people seem to struggle during the week of *yesod*.

IN A SENTENCE
When it's time to talk, make it happen. You may have to push some obstacles out of the way.

PRACTICE
Identify a relationship in which you struggle, but it is hard to see why, or one in which you see why, but are having a hard time communicating about it. Do your best to understand what the difficulties are. If you find your mind wandering – totally understandable, given how challenging this is – bring yourself back. Consider the best ways to explore those dynamics, and how some aspect of those dynamics could be addressed without doing damage to the relationship as a whole. And then, make it happen.

WEEK SIX DAY FOUR

Reflections

YEAR ONE

YEAR TWO

YEAR THREE

YEAR FOUR

YEAR FIVE

WEEK SIX DAY FIVE

*Hayom arba'im yom, she'hem chamisha shavuot
v'chamisha yamim la'omer*

HOD OF YESOD

There are times when we are moved to bring focus to one of the important relationships that populate our lives and we need to know more about whether and how it is working. We might need to have a serious conversation.

Put another way, we might think it's important to have a conversation about how things are going, and we may be right, and we'll have to push through some resistance – inner or outer – in order to have that conversation. That's *netzach* of *yesod*.

And the person with whom I feel the need to do some relationship work may not agree. And it may be that their reticence to have the conversation or do the work is not a function of resistance, but of a different view about what is happening – and what needs to happen – in the relationship. Honoring that is *hod* of *yesod*.

It may well be that my desire to engage is based on anxieties, unfair expectations, misunderstandings, impatience, and a whole slew of other factors that convince me that I need to push. My work today is to listen – to words spoken as well as more subtle communication – about the state of the relationship and what it may need.

IN A SENTENCE
Are you sure things need to change? What does the other person think?

PRACTICE
Tune into what your partners-in-relationship are telling you about how things are going. You may need to ask: are we good? While you're gathering intel on how this particular partner-in-relationship is thinking about the situation, also notice how that corresponds to your own views, and get curious about the gaps between your view and theirs.

WEEK SIX DAY FIVE

Reflections

YEAR ONE

YEAR TWO

YEAR THREE

YEAR FOUR

YEAR FIVE

WEEK SIX DAY SIX

Hayom echad v'arbaim yom, she'hem chamisha shavuot v'shisha yamim la'omer

YESOD OF YESOD

Yoseph – the paragon of *yesod* – does an incredible job of directing peoples' attention toward the relationships they live in. In light of repeated attempts at seduction from his master's wife, he reminds her that their relationship would have a huge impact on many other relationships. Throughout the ordeal with his brothers, disguised as the Egyptian viceroy, he repeatedly reminds them that the way they are in relationship somewhere is the way they are in relationship everywhere.

His early attempt at clarifying his relationship to his brothers – "listen to this dream I had!" – leads to hatred and bloodshed. By the time we reach the ordeal in Egypt, though, we see how refined he is, gently moving his brothers from realization to realization, until they finally see who they have been, and then are able to take a step forward.

It's not easy to move a relationship forward. It's also not easy to allow someone else to move your relationship forward. Healthy *yesod* of *yesod* manifests when both people can guide and be guided toward awareness, clarity, growth and movement.

IN A SENTENCE
What changes when you are or aren't the one to bring things up?

PRACTICE
Choose a relationship on which to focus. Notice how different moods, stimuli, comments, movements, gestures, times of day, activities, etc. affect the relationship. Which rules and limitations, potentials and possibilities of the relationship affect you most? What do you know about how the other person would answer these questions? How could this information help you move forward?

WEEK SIX DAY SIX

Reflections

YEAR ONE

YEAR TWO

YEAR THREE

YEAR FOUR

YEAR FIVE

WEEK SIX DAY SEVEN

Hayom shanim v'arbaim yom, she'hem shisha shavuot la'omer

MALCHUT OF YESOD

We are in so many relationships. And all of our relationships add up to One Relationship. Each individual relationship draws on the others, informs and is informed by all the others. The insights and inspirations – as well as frustrations and limitations – that show up in any given relationship are woven into the overarching tapestry of Relationship.

Occasionally we get to look at the entire tapestry, seeing how our relationships relate to each other, interact, interfere, obscure, obstruct, enhance, catalyze, facilitate, give meaning to, shed light on, complement and balance with each other. At such times, we may get a glimpse into the patterns of our relationships. This could give us an opportunity to celebrate ourselves – or make us want to hide under a rock.

Today we get to ask ourselves, how is our relationship to our relationships? And how is our relationship to Relationship? What are the patterns that span across many or all of our relationships? What might I want to start taking iterative actions toward changing?

IN A SENTENCE
What are some elements that show up in all your relationships?

PRACTICE
As relationship stuff pops up today, get curious about whether it is indicative of a larger pattern. Follow clues from one relationship to another, to see how those things play out on a larger scale. If you have access to such a resource, find someone with whom to reflect on those patterns, and see if you can get some insight into how to amplify the healthy, positive parts and work with the less glamorous ones.

WEEK SIX DAY SEVEN

Reflections

YEAR ONE

YEAR TWO

YEAR THREE

YEAR FOUR

YEAR FIVE

WEEK SEVEN

MALCHUT

WHEN WE TALK ABOUT God's *malchut*, we are describing the way in which God's will manifests in the details of the world we live in. In a true *malchut*, every detail of the experience of the 'kingdom' or 'queendom' points toward the 'king' or 'queen'. If they do not, then sovereignty has not been fully realized.

Rebbe Nachman writes that we are all charged with a particular 'sovereignty' or *malchut*. For some it is as vast as an entire team or project, or more; for others it is limited to self-advocacy or maintaining their own health and well-being. In either case, *malchut* implies responsibility.

So we are each responsible for *something*. Within that something we are fully responsible. When that particular domain is thriving, that is an indication of the strength of our *malchut*.

WEEK SEVEN DAY ONE

Hayom shlosha v'arbaim yom, she'hem shisha shavuot v'yom echad la'omer

CHESED OF MALCHUT

Responsibility should trump fear. Given that we each have a particular realm to oversee, maintain, and provide for, it is simply not an option to refuse to do so. Just as a sovereign should not neglect the needs of any part of their domain, we cannot neglect the needs of our own domains. If we do not accept our responsibility and take it seriously, people could suffer.

That said, it is not always obvious where our domain lies. We may not want to admit or accept responsibility for some areas, and we may want responsibility for other areas that are actually beyond our capacity at this time. So this trait implies taking full responsibility for the realm(s) that we know to be ours, and calls on us to move closer to other realms in an attempt to see if we have the right combination of vision, skills, and passion – and permission – to take leadership in that area as well.

King Saul, the first king of Israel, failed to take responsibility for his kingdom. When the time came for him to assert his kingship by completely vanquishing the tribe of Amalek, including livestock, he didn't follow through. When the prophet Samuel asked him why, he said, "The people spared the best of the livestock, in order to sacrifice them to God." Samuel disparagingly responded, "Even if you are small in your own eyes, you are the head of the tribes of Israel!"

IN A SENTENCE
Own the domains that are yours. Wonder if your domain is bigger than you thought.

PRACTICE
Consider the aspects and facets of the domains within which you operate that might be fully yours. Are you doing a good job of taking responsibility there? Be honest – are there some areas that you really are responsible for, but you are shirking that responsibility? Find a good way to indicate that you have ascended the throne of that realm. Some small action? A prayer? Is there an area where you think you might be called to responsibility? Step closer to that area and see what you find.

WEEK SEVEN DAY ONE

Reflections

YEAR ONE

YEAR TWO

YEAR THREE

YEAR FOUR

YEAR FIVE

WEEK SEVEN DAY TWO

Hayom arba'a v'arbaim yom, she'hem shisha shavuot ushnei yamim la'omer

GEVURAH OF MALCHUT

Everyone has times when they thought they should have — and did — take responsibility for something, and the project fizzled under their hand. This can happen for many reasons. One possibility is that it is simply not their domain.

We might wish it were our domain. That wish doesn't change anything. It might just point our attention away from, and cause us to neglect, a domain we should be tending to.

While it is imperative to take responsibility for the realms that are within our sovereignty, it is equally urgent to *not* take responsibility for those realms that are not. This requires an enormous amount of discipline and self-restraint — it is certainly tempting to try to have impact all over the map.

It takes real humility to cede *malchut* to someone else. When we see that someone is better equipped or more motivated to handle a situation than we are, we must consider giving it over, no matter how humbling it may be. Ability to do this indicates awareness of something larger than just my own sense of self-worth.

IN A SENTENCE
Don't take responsibility for a *malchut* that is clearly not yours.

PRACTICE
Identify an area of your life in which things don't seem to be going well. Ask yourself the hard question: which aspects or facets of this situation really are in your domain, and which are not? Find a good way to indicate letting go of those realms that are not under your auspices. Notice what comes up as you make some small act of letting go.

WEEK SEVEN DAY TWO

Reflections

YEAR ONE

YEAR TWO

YEAR THREE

YEAR FOUR

YEAR FIVE

WEEK SEVEN DAY THREE

Hayom chamisha v'arbaim yom, she'hem shisha shavuot ushelosha yamim la'omer

TIF'ERET OF MALCHUT

In geology, the meeting-point between two elements – say, quartz and impurities of iron – often produces beautiful results – in this case, amethyst. The same is true in music, cuisine, and art: as long as the multiple elements do not overwhelm each other, the interaction between them is often beautiful or intriguing, and amplifies the exceptional qualities of each.

The same is true where two human *malchuyot* (plural of *malchut*) meet. If the meeting between them is good-natured and well-managed – if each person effectively understands where their *malchut* ends and the next one begins – then the interaction between them can be something beautiful. *Tif'eret* of *malchut*.

Where multiple *malchuyot* border each other, beauty is possible. But that also may become a no-man's-land. It's where clashes – or mutual neglect – are more likely to happen. As we get closer to the border, more self-awareness and more communication are needed. Each of us is required to fine-tune their own sense of *tif'eret* in order for that beauty to emerge.

IN A SENTENCE
We each have a *malchut*. The interaction between our *malchuyot* can be beautiful if we work together.

PRACTICE
Notice a realm that is fully under your auspices. Say, your yard. See where your yard meets your neighbor's yard. Is it clear where one ends and the other begins? What does the meeting-place between them look like? Have you spoken about it? Is the conversation generous? Respectful? Do you walk away from it with a clear sense of how things will go? Ask these same questions about a less-terrestrial area of life where your responsibilities abut someone else's.

WEEK SEVEN DAY THREE

Reflections

YEAR ONE

YEAR TWO

YEAR THREE

YEAR FOUR

YEAR FIVE

WEEK SEVEN DAY FOUR

Hayom shisha v'arbaim yom, she'hem shisha shavuot v'arba'a yamim la'omer

NETZACH OF MALCHUT

What happens when someone or something infringes on an area that is within our *malchut*? We may have to draw clear lines. We may have to address miscommunication. We may have to use some amount of force to push them out. For a vivid example, consider what you would do if a stranger attempted to indoctrinate your child into an ideology without your permission.

Meanwhile, you might need to take a look at why this *malchut* appeared to be up for grabs. Did you make it clear that you were on it? Were you bringing the necessary level of attention and enthusiasm? Were you even paying attention? Do you have a vision for that *malchut*? Did you even know and accept that it is your *malchut*?

You might wonder: have I devoted enough time and attention to talking about big questions with my kids? What void did I leave, that was filled by another? When this concerns something precious – community, children, marriage – then *netzach* of *malchut* becomes urgent. Obstacles must be quickly navigated and action is required.

IN A SENTENCE
If someone is in your *malchut* and they shouldn't be, push them out. Use the right amount of force.

PRACTICE
Notice something that affects your life negatively. Try to think about each aspect of it as a level of domain, and figure out who is currently taking responsibility for each level of domain. Should that someone be you, or at least someone you select or trust? What accounts for the discrepancy between how it's going, and how you think it should be going? What could be done about it? What are the obstacles in the way of it getting done? Do you care enough to push through those obstacles?

WEEK SEVEN DAY FOUR

Reflections

YEAR ONE

YEAR TWO

YEAR THREE

YEAR FOUR

YEAR FIVE

WEEK SEVEN DAY FIVE

*Hayom shiva v'arbaim yom, she'hem shisha shavuot
v'chamisha yamim la'omer*

HOD OF MALCHUT

There is a (possibly offensive?) expression "too many chiefs and not enough Indians." As important as it is to take full responsibility for my own *malchut*, it is equally important to accept someone's else's true *malchut* in their own domain. And not just accept begrudgingly. When I am in that person's well-deserved *malchut*, I need to be ready to accept their leadership and guidance, willingly, without attitude or resentment.

So while *gevurah* of *malchut* requires restraining myself from taking *malchut* where it is inappropriate, *hod* of *malchut* concerns actively recognizing and respecting another's sovereignty in a realm that concerns me – enough to follow orders within it.

An additional dimension of *hod* of *malchut* parallels the reality that a Jewish king (*malchut*) would have a priest (*hod*, like Aaron) to guide them in the priestly matters of the kingdom. Similarly, it is essential to have people we can go to for sage advice about our own *malchuyot*, whether for personal support, insight on more pragmatic matters, or guidance concerning the religious elements that may be operative there.

IN A SENTENCE
If you're in someone else's *malchut*, let them call the shots.

PRACTICE
Look around. See how you, and people you care about, benefit from other *malchuyot* – be it God's or another person's. How do you show up in other *malchuyot*? Are you grateful? Jealous? Resentful? Does it make you feel inferior? And how good are you at allowing others to help you with your own *malchut*? Are you able to accept help without feeling like you're inferior for needing that help? Do you have a "religious advisor" for your *malchut*? Should you?

WEEK SEVEN DAY FIVE
Reflections

YEAR ONE

YEAR TWO

YEAR THREE

YEAR FOUR

YEAR FIVE

WEEK SEVEN DAY SIX

Hayom shmonah v'arbaim yom, she'hem shisha shavuot v'shisha yamim la'omer

YESOD OF MALCHUT

Within a particular domain—say, the project your team is working on—there are relationships. As you understand and take responsibility for your particular domain, you must work to strengthen the relationships within that domain. Beyond whether everyone knows their particular roles and where their roles share boundaries with other people's roles, the human relationships still need to be cared for.

Does everyone who is touched by your *malchut* feel like they can talk to you? Do they feel cared for? More importantly, do you they feel like you are doing it for you, or doing it for them? Many kings and queens see their domains as serving them, and not the reverse. At that point, *malchut* becomes exploitation.

In *yesod* of *malchut*, we are challenged to be powerful without being grandiose. We must embrace the primary function of *malchut*, which is to provide, care, and defend. This will be indicated by the human connections within that *malchut*. But when the relationship is rigged to serve only us, then this is a flaw in *yesod* of *malchut*. And that, too, will be indicated by those human connections.

IN A SENTENCE
How are the relationships within your *malchut*?

PRACTICE
Take the time to acknowledge and strengthen the relationships within your *malchut*. Do your children feel they are being taken care of? Subordinates at work? Is your home well cared for? Ask around. Take feedback seriously.

WEEK SEVEN DAY SIX

Reflections

YEAR ONE

YEAR TWO

YEAR THREE

YEAR FOUR

YEAR FIVE

WEEK SEVEN DAY SEVEN

Hayom tisha v'arbaim yom, she'hem shiv'a shavuot la'omer

MALCHUT OF MALCHUT

Malchut is a tree. A twig has *malchut* concerning the leaves that grow off of it. A branch has *malchut* concerning the twigs that extend from it. And the trunk has *malchut* concerning the branches that emerge from it.

This makes for a tricky balance. My *malchut* must be solid enough to provide structure and support for what it holds, and fluid enough to be open to the *malchut* within which it operates.

Even a Jewish king's *malchut* is not the trunk. It is, or should be, a manifestation of God's *malchut*. It should point toward its Source. Ultimately, it is one more element that must be harmonious and cooperative with all other elements.

If my domain is clearly an element of God's domain, I have succeeded in *malchut* of *malchut*. I have made a channel to God's will, and a place where it can easily manifest.

IN A SENTENCE
What is the bigger *malchut* in which your *malchut* operates? Do they connect well?

PRACTICE
Is your domain all about you, or does it acknowledge a higher purpose and a larger context? Spend a moment considering a larger *malchut* that nests your *malchut* and the *malchuyot* that nest within yours. How is the flow between them all?

You have finished counting the Omer! The 50th gate opens tomorrow on Shavuot. May all the work we have done serve as a conduit for the light of the Torah, and may the light of the Torah infuse all of our relationships with joy, purpose, and holiness.

WEEK SEVEN DAY SEVEN

Reflections

YEAR ONE

YEAR TWO

YEAR THREE

YEAR FOUR

YEAR FIVE

COUNTING

בָּרוּךְ אַתָּה יְהֹוָה אֱלֹהֵינוּ מֶלֶךְ הָעוֹלָם. אֲשֶׁר קִדְּשָׁנוּ בְּמִצְוֹתָיו וְצִוָּנוּ עַל סְפִירַת הָעֹמֶר:
baruch atah Ado-nai Elo-heinu melech ha'olam
asher kideshanu b'mitz'vo'tav ve'tzi'vanu al sefirat ha'omer

1. הַיּוֹם יוֹם אֶחָד, לָעוֹמֶר: *Today is one day of the Omer*
2. הַיּוֹם שְׁנֵי יָמִים, לָעוֹמֶר:
3. הַיּוֹם שְׁלֹשָׁה יָמִים, לָעוֹמֶר:
4. הַיּוֹם אַרְבָּעָה יָמִים, לָעוֹמֶר:
5. הַיּוֹם חֲמִשָּׁה יָמִים, לָעוֹמֶר:
6. הַיּוֹם שִׁשָּׁה יָמִים, לָעוֹמֶר:
7. הַיּוֹם שִׁבְעָה יָמִים שֶׁהֵם שָׁבוּעַ אֶחָד, לָעוֹמֶר:
8. הַיּוֹם שְׁמוֹנָה יָמִים שֶׁהֵם שָׁבוּעַ אֶחָד וְיוֹם אֶחָד, לָעוֹמֶר: *Today is 8 days of the Omer, which is 1 week and 1 day*
9. הַיּוֹם תִּשְׁעָה יָמִים שֶׁהֵם שָׁבוּעַ אֶחָד וּשְׁנֵי יָמִים, לָעוֹמֶר:
10. הַיּוֹם עֲשָׂרָה יָמִים שֶׁהֵם שָׁבוּעַ אֶחָד וּשְׁלֹשָׁה יָמִים, לָעוֹמֶר:
11. הַיּוֹם אַחַד עָשָׂר יוֹם שֶׁהֵם שָׁבוּעַ אֶחָד וְאַרְבָּעָה יָמִים, לָעוֹמֶר:
12. הַיּוֹם שְׁנֵים עָשָׂר יוֹם שֶׁהֵם שָׁבוּעַ אֶחָד וַחֲמִשָּׁה יָמִים, לָעוֹמֶר:
13. הַיּוֹם שְׁלֹשָׁה עָשָׂר יוֹם שֶׁהֵם שָׁבוּעַ אֶחָד וְשִׁשָּׁה יָמִים, לָעוֹמֶר:
14. הַיּוֹם אַרְבָּעָה עָשָׂר יוֹם שֶׁהֵם שְׁנֵי שָׁבוּעוֹת, לָעוֹמֶר: *Today is 14 days of the Omer, which is 2 weeks*
15. הַיּוֹם חֲמִשָּׁה עָשָׂר יוֹם שֶׁהֵם שְׁנֵי שָׁבוּעוֹת וְיוֹם אֶחָד, לָעוֹמֶר:
16. הַיּוֹם שִׁשָּׁה עָשָׂר יוֹם שֶׁהֵם שְׁנֵי שָׁבוּעוֹת וּשְׁנֵי יָמִים, לָעוֹמֶר:
17. הַיּוֹם שִׁבְעָה עָשָׂר יוֹם שֶׁהֵם שְׁנֵי שָׁבוּעוֹת וּשְׁלֹשָׁה יָמִים, לָעוֹמֶר:
18. הַיּוֹם שְׁמוֹנָה עָשָׂר יוֹם שֶׁהֵם שְׁנֵי שָׁבוּעוֹת וְאַרְבָּעָה יָמִים, לָעוֹמֶר:
19. הַיּוֹם תִּשְׁעָה עָשָׂר יוֹם שֶׁהֵם שְׁנֵי שָׁבוּעוֹת וַחֲמִשָּׁה יָמִים, לָעוֹמֶר:
20. הַיּוֹם עֶשְׂרִים יוֹם שֶׁהֵם שְׁנֵי שָׁבוּעוֹת וְשִׁשָּׁה יָמִים, לָעוֹמֶר:
21. הַיּוֹם אֶחָד וְעֶשְׂרִים יוֹם שֶׁהֵם שְׁלֹשָׁה שָׁבוּעוֹת, לָעוֹמֶר:
22. הַיּוֹם שְׁנַיִם וְעֶשְׂרִים יוֹם שֶׁהֵם שְׁלֹשָׁה שָׁבוּעוֹת וְיוֹם אֶחָד, לָעוֹמֶר:
23. הַיּוֹם שְׁלֹשָׁה וְעֶשְׂרִים יוֹם שֶׁהֵם שְׁלֹשָׁה שָׁבוּעוֹת וּשְׁנֵי יָמִים, לָעוֹמֶר:
24. הַיּוֹם אַרְבָּעָה וְעֶשְׂרִים יוֹם שֶׁהֵם שְׁלֹשָׁה שָׁבוּעוֹת וּשְׁלֹשָׁה יָמִים, לָעוֹמֶר:
25. הַיּוֹם חֲמִשָּׁה וְעֶשְׂרִים יוֹם שֶׁהֵם שְׁלֹשָׁה שָׁבוּעוֹת וְאַרְבָּעָה יָמִים, לָעוֹמֶר:
26. הַיּוֹם שִׁשָּׁה וְעֶשְׂרִים יוֹם שֶׁהֵם שְׁלֹשָׁה שָׁבוּעוֹת וַחֲמִשָּׁה יָמִים, לָעוֹמֶר:
27. הַיּוֹם שִׁבְעָה וְעֶשְׂרִים יוֹם שֶׁהֵם שְׁלֹשָׁה שָׁבוּעוֹת וְשִׁשָּׁה יָמִים, לָעוֹמֶר:
28. הַיּוֹם שְׁמוֹנָה וְעֶשְׂרִים יוֹם שֶׁהֵם אַרְבָּעָה שָׁבוּעוֹת, לָעוֹמֶר:
29. הַיּוֹם תִּשְׁעָה וְעֶשְׂרִים יוֹם שֶׁהֵם אַרְבָּעָה שָׁבוּעוֹת וְיוֹם אֶחָד, לָעוֹמֶר:
30. הַיּוֹם שְׁלֹשִׁים יוֹם שֶׁהֵם אַרְבָּעָה שָׁבוּעוֹת וּשְׁנֵי יָמִים, לָעוֹמֶר:
31. הַיּוֹם אֶחָד וּשְׁלֹשִׁים יוֹם שֶׁהֵם אַרְבָּעָה שָׁבוּעוֹת וּשְׁלֹשָׁה יָמִים, לָעוֹמֶר:
32. הַיּוֹם שְׁנַיִם וּשְׁלֹשִׁים יוֹם שֶׁהֵם אַרְבָּעָה שָׁבוּעוֹת וְאַרְבָּעָה יָמִים, לָעוֹמֶר:
33. הַיּוֹם שְׁלֹשָׁה וּשְׁלֹשִׁים יוֹם שֶׁהֵם אַרְבָּעָה שָׁבוּעוֹת וַחֲמִשָּׁה יָמִים, לָעוֹמֶר:
34. הַיּוֹם אַרְבָּעָה וּשְׁלֹשִׁים יוֹם שֶׁהֵם אַרְבָּעָה שָׁבוּעוֹת וְשִׁשָּׁה יָמִים, לָעוֹמֶר:
35. הַיּוֹם חֲמִשָּׁה וּשְׁלֹשִׁים יוֹם שֶׁהֵם חֲמִשָּׁה שָׁבוּעוֹת, לָעוֹמֶר:
36. הַיּוֹם שִׁשָּׁה וּשְׁלֹשִׁים יוֹם שֶׁהֵם חֲמִשָּׁה שָׁבוּעוֹת וְיוֹם אֶחָד, לָעוֹמֶר:
37. הַיּוֹם שִׁבְעָה וּשְׁלֹשִׁים יוֹם שֶׁהֵם חֲמִשָּׁה שָׁבוּעוֹת וּשְׁנֵי יָמִים, לָעוֹמֶר:
38. הַיּוֹם שְׁמוֹנָה וּשְׁלֹשִׁים יוֹם שֶׁהֵם חֲמִשָּׁה שָׁבוּעוֹת וּשְׁלֹשָׁה יָמִים, לָעוֹמֶר:
39. הַיּוֹם תִּשְׁעָה וּשְׁלֹשִׁים יוֹם שֶׁהֵם חֲמִשָּׁה שָׁבוּעוֹת וְאַרְבָּעָה יָמִים, לָעוֹמֶר:
40. הַיּוֹם אַרְבָּעִים יוֹם שֶׁהֵם חֲמִשָּׁה שָׁבוּעוֹת וַחֲמִשָּׁה יָמִים, לָעוֹמֶר:
41. הַיּוֹם אֶחָד וְאַרְבָּעִים יוֹם שֶׁהֵם חֲמִשָּׁה שָׁבוּעוֹת וְשִׁשָּׁה יָמִים, לָעוֹמֶר:
42. הַיּוֹם שְׁנַיִם וְאַרְבָּעִים יוֹם שֶׁהֵם שִׁשָּׁה שָׁבוּעוֹת, לָעוֹמֶר:
43. הַיּוֹם שְׁלֹשָׁה וְאַרְבָּעִים יוֹם שֶׁהֵם שִׁשָּׁה שָׁבוּעוֹת וְיוֹם אֶחָד, לָעוֹמֶר:
44. הַיּוֹם אַרְבָּעָה וְאַרְבָּעִים יוֹם שֶׁהֵם שִׁשָּׁה שָׁבוּעוֹת וּשְׁנֵי יָמִים, לָעוֹמֶר:
45. הַיּוֹם חֲמִשָּׁה וְאַרְבָּעִים יוֹם שֶׁהֵם שִׁשָּׁה שָׁבוּעוֹת וּשְׁלֹשָׁה יָמִים, לָעוֹמֶר:
46. הַיּוֹם שִׁשָּׁה וְאַרְבָּעִים יוֹם שֶׁהֵם שִׁשָּׁה שָׁבוּעוֹת וְאַרְבָּעָה יָמִים, לָעוֹמֶר:
47. הַיּוֹם שִׁבְעָה וְאַרְבָּעִים יוֹם שֶׁהֵם שִׁשָּׁה שָׁבוּעוֹת וַחֲמִשָּׁה יָמִים, לָעוֹמֶר:
48. הַיּוֹם שְׁמוֹנָה וְאַרְבָּעִים יוֹם שֶׁהֵם שִׁשָּׁה שָׁבוּעוֹת וְשִׁשָּׁה יָמִים, לָעוֹמֶר:
49. הַיּוֹם תִּשְׁעָה וְאַרְבָּעִים יוֹם שֶׁהֵם שִׁבְעָה שָׁבוּעוֹת, לָעוֹמֶר:

ABOUT THE AUTHOR

Gavriel Goldfeder attended the Bat Ayin Yeshiva, where he was ordained. He spent a decade at Aish Kodesh in Boulder, Colorado, six years at MIT Hillel, and currently teaches at the Gann Academy. Along the way, he has developed a unique voice in conveying the practical wisdom of Jewish life with humor, depth, and cultural savvy.

In addition to his day job, Gavriel produces a podcast (a.k.a. rabbi), runs a publishing house (Alternadox Press), and writes vociferously. You can find more about him and his work at www.realrabbi.com.

The art work gracing the cover is by Avraham Lowenthal of the Tzfat Gallery of Mystical Art, in Northern Israel. His work can be seen at www.kabbalahart.com. The original painting has been modified for this cover.

www.ingramcontent.com/pod-product-compliance
Lightning Source LLC
Chambersburg PA
CBHW062111290426
44110CB00023B/2781